Feminists Among Us

This book is number nine in the Series on Gender and Sexuality in Information Studies, Emily Drabinski, series editor.

Also in the series:

Feminist Reference Desk: Concepts, Critiques, and Conversations,
edited by Maria T. Accardi

Queer Library Alliance: Global Reflections and Imaginings
edited by Rae-Anne Montague and Lucas McKeever

*Queers Online: LGBT Digital Practices in Libraries,
Archives, and Museums*
edited by Rachel Wexelbaum

Ephemeral Material: Queering the Archive
by Alana Kumbier

Feminist and Queer Information Studies Reader
edited by Rebecca Dean and Patrick Keilty

Feminist Pedagogy for Library Instruction
by Maria Accardi

*Make Your Own History: Documenting Feminist and
Queer Activism in the 21st Century*
edited by Lyz Bly and Kelly Wooten

Out Behind the Desk: Workplace Issues for LGBTQ Librarians
edited by Tracy Nectoux

Feminists Among Us

Resistance and Advocacy in Library Leadership

Edited by
Shirley Lew and Baharak Yousefi

Library Juice Press
Sacramento, CA

Published by Library Juice Press in 2017

Library Juice Press
PO Box 188784
Sacramento, CA 95818

http://libraryjuicepress.com

This book is printed on acid-free, sustainably-sourced paper.

Library of Congress Cataloging
in Publication data pending.

Table of Content

FOREWORD

It's an extraordinary time to be in the field of information studies, with librarians taking up some of the most pressing social and political issues of our time. Regularly, we now see librarians and information & communication workers engaging with, and attempting to transform, systems of racialization and gender that are inextricably intersectional. With deliberate efforts to organize and advocate, many who work in our fields have sharpened their focus on how power and oppression must be addressed, and dare I say, dismantled, in order to realize the most ideal visions of a democratic, pluralistic, and socially just society. This book is a commitment to thinking through multiple dimensions of putting feminist values into practice. It is timely, and crucial to amplifying the concerns that many of us share about reimagining the role of librarians and information professionals as workers central to social transformation.

The inimitable scholar and activist, Dr. Angela Y. Davis' words about the importance of feminism have remarkable resonance to me as I think about the critical work we are trying to advance in the fields of information studies. She characterizes feminism this way:

> Feminism involves so much more than gender equality and it involves so much more than gender. Feminism must involve consciousness of capitalism (I mean the feminism that I relate to, and there are multiple feminisms, right). So it has to involve a consciousness of capitalism and racism and colonialism and post-colonialities, and ability and more genders than we can even imagine and more sexualities than we ever thought we could name.[1]

---

1 Angela Y. Davis, "Feminism and Abolition: Theories and Practices for the 21st Century" (lecture, CSRPC Annual Public Lecture and CSGS Classics in Feminist Theory Series, Chicago, IL, May 3, 2013).

These principles, or organizing logics, can be powerfully engaged among those who are responsible for so many dimensions of information and knowledge dissemination, curation, discovery, access, archiving, and preservation. Where Angela reminds us that many forms of feminism can give us a consciousness to name multiple forms of oppression, it can also liberate us, and provoke us to imagine, and name, a multiplicity of new possibilities.

This "power to name," or make visible (or obscure), or amplify voices and communities has been the clarion call of our scholarly mentor and colleague, Dr. Hope Olson, from the University of Wisconsin, Milwaukee. I think of her work, and the ways that explicitly naming the power that librarians and archivists hold in stewarding and interpreting knowledge as I write this foreword, knowing our field is anything but neutral. An important source of our power is in the many feminisms we embrace and put into practice. This book, then, is a guide in how to envision feminist practice in library and information studies. It is full of stories, and critiques, and inspiration for how to enact feminism across multiple types of information work. It may be a brand new roadmap for some, and for others, a reminder that a protracted struggle for socially just work continues. I believe that ultimately, this book is a source of possibility and a resource to assist us in seeing how we can do our work better.

As some of the authors in this book note, the field of librarianship is highly feminized, and it is mostly engaged in by white cis-women. On these terms, this is both problematic and full of possibilities for addressing feminism at both the structural and individual levels. Structurally, the lack of a multi-racial and transgendered field is a severe limitation for broadening participation among those who might have tacit interest and commitment to anti-racist, feminist, and postcolonial work in the field; knowledge which is likely to be brought to bear from the fields of black studies, ethnic studies, and gender studies. Lived experience and academic preparation allow us to think about interventions in the field that stem from thoughtful engagement with intersectional theories of gender, class, and race. It allows us to build solidarities across multiple axes and enact the kind of change we want to see in society. In this regard, our field is woefully under-engaged in this kind of interdisciplinary work, although many of us are trying to foreground these epistemologies in our rigorous academic research and professional training of the next generation of library and information professionals.

The structural interventions that feminism might provide could profoundly transform society for the better: we might see expanded access to public goods like libraries and archives, funding and support for educational and media institutions, affordable and accessible health care, social inclusion and security for the most vulnerable and historically disenfranchised among us, affordable housing, and expanded social services. Undoubtedly, there would be an important role for information workers to foment these visions, work that should we not do, nor take seriously, will equally contribute to the erosion of our fragile and yet to be fully realized experiment in democracy in the United States. At the individual level, we might ask ourselves how a profession so profoundly feminized, so explicitly dominated by women, is not typically characterized as a "feminist profession?" It begs a series of questions: what stands in the way of a field that is more than 80% women of holding up feminism as a core value? What does the field put at stake when it chooses to not explicitly take up an intersectional feminist stance in its practice and identity? What are the "possessive investments," as framed by the field of critical whiteness studies and the work of professor George Lipsitz, in the fields of information and communication, and how could feminism disrupt those investments to work in a more organized manner in the interests of many genders, sexualities, ethnicities and cultures as a contribution to creating a more socially just society for all?

These are audacious goals, and I commend Shirley Lew and Baharak Yousefi for assembling a collection of important voices from our field who are committed to feminist praxis in library and information studies. I am honored to lend a voice, and encourage researchers, instructors, and practitioners to teach and learn from these pages. I hope that practitioners and researchers in the field of information studies will take up the challenge to introspect on the values we hold, and imagine new possibilities for transforming our fields, and the communities within which we belong, toward shared values that can remedy and repair the inequalities and injustices of our society. Certainly, there are "feminists among us" who will be inspired by this collection, and will forge new pathways to the future.

Safiya Umoja Noble, Ph.D.
University of California, Los Angeles

REFERENCES

Davis, Angela Y. "Feminism and Abolition: Theories and Practices for the 21st Century." Lecture, CSRPC Annual Public Lecture and CSGS Classics in Feminist Theory Series, Chicago, IL, May 3, 2013.

ACKNOWLEDGEMENTS

Situated in Vancouver, Canada, we acknowledge that we are settlers on unceded lands of Musqueam, Skwxwú7mesh, and Tsleil-Waututh peoples, and as we set out to reflect on resistance and advocacy in our work, we are mindful that libraries are part of the present and past colonial violence in North America. Decolonization work is central to our understanding of intersectional feminist praxis.

Our deepest gratitude to the contributors for the passion, generosity, and intelligence that you brought to your work in this book. This volume would not exist without your labour.

Our heartfelt thanks to everyone who read and provided us with insight and encouragement on the many drafts of the chapters we each wrote. Thank you Matthew Beall, Annette DeFaveri, Ania Dymarz, Ben Hyman, Cathy Kasper, Dale McCartney, Kathryn McNaughton, Keshav Mukunda, Lachlan Murray, Anne Olsen, Noël Patten, Hazel Plante, and David Ray Vance. Of course, all errors and shortcomings are our own.

Emily Drabinski, Series Editor extraordinaire, has been a wonderful source of support and inspiration along the way. Thank you, Emily. Our thanks also to Rory Litwin for the opportunity to publish with Library Juice Press and for providing this platform for critical perspectives and voices in librarianship.

We are grateful to Simon Fraser University and Vancouver Community College for supporting us in this endeavour.

Lastly, our love and gratitude to our wonderful families, friends, mentors, and communities. We are grateful for your guidance, your kindness, and for sustaining us always.

Shirley Lew and Baharak Yousefi
Vancouver, BC, Canada

Introduction

Shirley Lew and Baharak Yousefi

In March 2015, we travelled together from Vancouver, BC to Portland, OR to attend the first Critlib[1] Unconference as well as the Association of College and Research Libraries (ACRL) Conference. At that time, we were both working in middle management positions in academic libraries and had had ongoing conversations about our experiences and our understanding of the state of library leadership in North America. Over the years, the specific topics of discussion had varied but the themes remained fairly consistent: we wanted our work to be grounded in principles of care, cooperation, social justice, and anti-oppression. In short, it has been important to us to live and work as feminists as well as we know how. Our politics have also foregrounded our concerns around a variety of issues including demographics of librarians and library managers in Canada and the United States; neoliberal pressures and the impact of corporatization on our work, systems, and institutions; and employment precarity. At both the Unconference and the Conference, we spoke with colleagues with similar concerns and interests who did not see library management as part of their career trajectory. We found that their reasons for ruling out work in library administration were profoundly political. Often our colleagues saw an irreconcilable gap between occupying these named positions of power and their personal and professional politics.

---

1 Critlib is short for "critical librarianship," a movement of library workers committed to bringing critical perspectives based on social justice principles into their work and the practice of librarianship.

At the same time, many demonstrate tremendous leadership in the profession through their work as scholars, practitioners, activists, and organizers. While we understood and empathized with this position, we were also quick to make arguments in favor of taking on management work with the intent of change-making. We gave examples of colleagues who foreground inclusion, transparency, care, and collective decision-making in their work as managers and talked about the ways in which they resist the status quo and advocate on behalf of their staff and communities. We argued that a grounding in feminist or other progressive politics is precisely what is needed in library leadership today. *Feminists Among Us* is a continuation of those conversations and aims to add the voices of feminist library and information studies professionals and researchers who engage critically with both management work and librarianship. We hope that by collecting these accounts of professional acts, interactions, and dynamics and naming them as explicitly feminist, the chapters that follow document aspects of an existing community of practice as well as invite fellow feminists, advocates, and resisters to consider library leadership as a career path.

The chapters in this collection reflect a range of perspectives in the LIS community, coming from different places of practice, roles, and personal and professional experiences that make up a feminist praxis. This volume includes the voices of librarians who are leading by working in a named position of leadership in a library, by advocating for change in their writing and scholarship, and by consciously behaving and engaging differently in their workplaces. All contributors are feminists, bringing to their accounts varied experiences of gender discrimination intersected with race, class, sexuality, and other social categories that are oppressed in patriarchal systems of power and organization.

The authors have written about feminist leadership in different ways about a range of topics. The book opens with chapters by Maura Smale and Shirley Lew, both of whom explore their roles as feminist leaders in libraries through personal narrative and reflection. In their chapters, they trace their path to both feminism and leadership and discuss what these concepts mean to them, and how they sustain their feminist praxis in their lives, their work, and their communities. These are followed by three chapters by Lisa Richmond, Shana Higgins, and Baharak Yousefi, who approach the topic from a theoretical perspective, drawing upon critical theory frameworks from various disciplines to engage with and interrogate assumptions about our professional values as related to actual practice and notions of effective leadership. Lisa Richmond examines feminization of the profession in the context of academic libraries and library leadership and argues that the philosophy of servant leadership, viewed as appropriate for library leaders, is problematically gendered with feminine-coded attributes and can negatively impact the perception of the value of academic libraries on campus and the effectiveness of female leaders in libraries. In her chapter, Shana Higgins takes the view that the feminization of our profession has associated values that are essential to the work we do in libraries, and referring to feminist critical theories, she further demonstrates how feminized-coded values are therefore often dismissed and marginalized as less vital in society. Baharak Yousefi takes yet a different approach, delving into Keller Easterling's concept of infrastructure space to probe the discrepancies between what we state to be our core purpose and values and what we actually do in libraries.

In the following two chapters, the first co-authored by Rachel Fleming and Kelly McBride and the second co-authored by Dale Askey and Jennifer Askey, the authors provocatively challenge libraries to do and be better. In their piece, Fleming and McBride write from a place of intersectional identities, disclosing the lack of honest discussion and action around diversity and inclusion in libraries and the role library leaders must play in creating change. Askey and Askey focus on the siloed cultures of library service and library IT, calling out the closed, impenetrable cultures of these worlds. They propose ways to bring about meaningful change by welcoming new skills, voices, and perspectives to our work.

The book closes with two chapters featuring interviews with feminist leaders in libraries. April Hathcock and Jennifer Vinopal use feminist research methodologies to interview eleven library leaders. They document the responses and themes that emerged from the interviews and discuss how feminism informs the work of these leaders. The last chapter is Tara Robertson's transcript of her conversation with Chris Bourg, Director of Libraries at MIT, in which Chris reflects on feminism and leadership, referring to personal and professional experiences from her time in military service to how she balances conflicting dynamics of workplace politics and her personal values. Bourg's thoughts and reflections tie together many of the ideas and questions raised throughout the book.

The process of working on this book with the chapter contributors and with each other has been a process of community-making and affirmation. As feminists committed to social justice, we are humbled and heartened by the work described in these pages and acknowledge that the refusal to accept the legitimacy of the status quo requires a tremendous amount of effort, courage, and resilience. This anthology is not a comprehensive account of feminist work or feminist leadership in libraries, but rather a collective attempt at capturing the hope and possibility of a way forward. Above all else, this book is an act of optimism. Lauren Berlant defines optimism "as the force that moves you out of yourself and into the world in order to bring closer the satisfying *something* that you cannot generate on your own but sense in the wake of a person, a way of life, an object, project, concept, or scene."[2] We cannot generate a way forward on our own but sense it—gladly—in our feminist communities.

---

2 Lauren Berlant, *Cruel Optimism* (Durham: Duke University Press, 2011).

REFERENCES

Berlant, Lauren. *Cruel Optimism*. Durham: Duke University Press, 2011.

Always a Novice: Feminist Learning and Leadership Practice

Maura A. Smale

Learning about the theory and practice of intersectional feminism played an important role in my development as a librarian and a library director, and the ongoing study of feminism continues to be integral to my leadership work. The definition of feminism that I prefer is the concise and powerful statement by bell hooks: "feminism seeks to end sexism, sexist exploitation, and oppression."[1] While I did not attend a library and information science graduate program with the express intention of becoming a library director, that is where I find myself. And while I have always considered myself a feminist, I had never studied feminism until recently and I am still new to feminist theory and practice. In sharing my experiences of embracing a novice mindset I hope to encourage others who support feminism—and especially intersectional feminist practice—to consider a leadership path in libraries.

From Academic Librarianship to Critical Pedagogy to Feminism

Like many librarians my path to this career was not direct. I returned to graduate school for my Master of Library and Information Science (MLIS) after having worked as an archaeologist and in online publishing. While in graduate school I took on a few different

---

1 bell hooks, *Feminism Is for Everybody* (Cambridge, MA: South End Press, 2000), vii.

internships—at a public research library, at a private university library, and at the library at Brooklyn College, part of the City University of New York (CUNY). Though by that time I had lived in New York City for fifteen years, I did not know much about CUNY before my internship at Brooklyn College. New York State education law states that the university has a "commitment to academic excellence and to the provision of equal access and opportunity for students, faculty and staff from all ethnic and racial groups and from both sexes," and that CUNY "is of vital importance as a vehicle for the upward mobility of the disadvantaged in the City of New York."[2] At Brooklyn College the library faculty and staff were dedicated and engaged, as were the students, drawn from across all boroughs of New York City. When I finished my degree and began to look for jobs I was especially interested in working at CUNY, and was delighted to be hired as Instruction Coordinator at New York City College of Technology (City Tech) in 2008.

As I immersed myself in instruction and reference in my new position, I also immersed myself in learning more about information literacy. In reading the professional literature, I found James Elmborg's and Michelle Holschuh-Simmons' articles about critical information literacy to be particularly compelling,[3] which encouraged me to create more opportunities for students to think critically about information in my instruction sessions. Reading Paolo Freire's *Pedagogy of the Oppressed* introduced me to critical pedagogy and I expanded my efforts to bring these ideas into my library classroom.[4] When I was approached by faculty in another department at City Tech who were developing a new degree program and were interested in a course on research and documentation for their students, I realized that this was an opportunity to develop a semester-length course with a focus on more than library skills. With the increased time with students we

---

2 "Mission & History," City University of New York, accessed August 13, 2016, http://www2.cuny.edu/about/history.

3 James Elmborg, "Critical Information Literacy: Implications for Instructional Practice," *The Journal of Academic Librarianship* 32, no. 2 (2006): 192-199; and Michelle Holschuh-Simmons, "Librarians as Disciplinary Discourse Mediators: Using Genre Theory to Move Toward Critical Information Literacy," *portal: Libraries & the Academy* 5, no. 3 (2005): 297-311.

4 Paulo Freire, *Pedagogy of the Oppressed*, 30th anniversary ed. (New York: Continuum, 2000).

could explore information issues like access, privacy, and ethics, and bring in students' lived experiences with research and information use.[5] Valuing students' experiences, engaging in active learning and group work, and making space for students to contribute to and shape their classroom experiences—all are feminist pedagogical practices that I was developing.[6]

Reading, practicing, and thinking about critical information literacy led me to realize that, while I had long identified as a feminist, I had never engaged in any intentional learning about feminism or feminist theory. In early 2014, I picked up hooks' *Feminism Is For Everybody*. As hooks notes in its early pages, her intent in writing was to produce "a straightforward, clear book —easy to read without being simplistic,"[7] a promise to herself and her readers that she keeps. Many of my college and graduate courses in the social sciences and humanities had required me to read theoretical texts heavy with academic terminology and jargon, with which I had often struggled. While the value of theory I can apply to my practice is readily apparent, I have always found it more difficult to read and analyze theory that is more abstract. I prefer readings that consider practice along with theory more explicitly, and reading hooks' book was the first step in acknowledging and addressing the gap in my knowledge about feminist theory.

I began to learn more about critical librarianship, a topic that encompasses critical information literacy and feminist library practice among other themes. In April 2014, several librarians founded the #critlib chats on the social media platform Twitter to discuss topics in critical librarianship.[8] A Twitter chat, which typically consists of one or more moderators posting questions for participants to answer while using a hashtag to identify the conversation, can sometimes be a challenging venue for focused and involved discussion of a multifaceted topic like critical librarianship. However, Twitter chats

---

5 Anne Leonard and Maura A. Smale, "The Three Credit Solution: Social Justice in an Information Literacy Course," in *Information Literacy and Social Justice*, ed. Lua Gregory and Shana Higgins (Sacramento, CA: Library Juice Press, 2013), 143-161.

6 Maria T. Accardi, *Feminist Pedagogy for Library Instruction* (Sacramento, CA: Library Juice Press, 2013), 50-52.

7 hooks, Feminism Is For Everybody, vii.

8 "Critlib Twitter Chats," accessed August 13, 2016, http://critlib.org/twitter-chats.

can be a valuable opportunity to engage in and follow the conversation with librarians across and beyond the U.S. and Canada, and I have been (and continue to be) an eager participant in the #critlib chats.[9] While I had been a Twitter user for several years, the #critlib chats mark the beginning of my own more intentional use of this social media platform as a professional development resource, especially for learning about feminism and anti-racism.

Around the same time, the U.S. and global news media increasingly began to report on the killings of people of color—especially black boys and men—by police and others. In the news and on Twitter, I followed the protests after the 2012 shooting of Trayvon Martin and the 2014 shooting of Michael Brown, sadly only two among many deaths, and the rise of the #BlackLivesMatter movement for racial justice. It became clear to me that as a white person in the United States I am complicit in what Mariana Ortega has called loving, knowing ignorance: "an ignorance of the thought and experience of women of color that is accompanied by both alleged love for and alleged knowledge about them."[10] My white privilege meant that I didn't know what I didn't know about the experiences of people of color, and I began to expand my study to include intersectional feminism, racism, and white supremacy.

Understanding Myself as a White Woman and a Feminist

I have identified as a feminist since my teen years, though throughout my early adulthood I was not drawn to feminism as a topic of academic (or extracurricular) study. I am sure that my privilege is the reason: I am a white, straight, cisgender, able-bodied, non-religious woman from a middle-class background. As a child I attended a mix of public, Catholic, and private schools, and my family and I predominantly lived in urban and suburban areas of the Northeastern U.S. in communities that were primarily though not exclusively white. I went directly

---

9 Maura A. Smale, "Beyond Livetweeting: Twitter Chats for Professional Development," *ACRLog* (blog), April 21, 2014. http://acrlog.org/2014/04/21/beyond-livetweeting-twitter-chats-for-professional-development.

10 Mariana Ortega, "Being Lovingly, Knowingly Ignorant: White Feminism and Women of Color," *Hypatia* 21, no. 3 (2006), 57.

from high school to college to a graduate program in anthropology, specializing in archaeology. After finishing my degree, I spent a few years working in online media before returning to graduate school for a Master of Library and Information Science, and have worked in academic libraries ever since. I was able to undertake several unpaid internships during my MLIS studies—essential experience, as I had not previously worked in a library—because I was fortunate enough to have a partner who could temporarily sustain our household on one income.

Though I have spent most of my life in academic environments, I have never taken a course in women's or gender studies and have not read most of the foundational feminist texts. My choice not to pursue coursework in feminism or feminist theory in college and graduate school was less a decision than a non-decision, and though it is something I regret, it is difficult to remember the specifics after twenty-five years. I suspect that my lack of engagement with feminist theory during my academic work stems from my experiences growing up in mostly white spaces in which I absorbed the lessons of white feminism from the 1960s and 1970s. I have never felt that I had to wear makeup or dress in an overtly feminine way if I preferred otherwise, and I was never dissuaded from studying archaeology, a predominantly male field. I think that I did not feel compelled to seek out intentional learning about feminism because as a white, middle-class woman, I was already benefitting from white feminism.

I also did not take courses in feminist theory in my library and information science program. More than two decades ago Jane Anne Hannigan stressed the value of studying feminist theory throughout the LIS curriculum, since the "basic premises upon which librarianship and information science have been built are structured on white, middle-class, male paradigms that have systematically, if unconsciously, silenced and excluded women."[11] The program I attended, like many programs, did not offer much LIS theory or history, which I now realize would have been especially valuable given the many problematic aspects of the history (and present state) of librarianship. As Todd Honma has noted, "from its very inception,

---

11 Jane Anne Hannigan, "A Feminist Standpoint for Library and Information Science Education," *Journal of Education for Library and Information Science* 35, no. 4 (1994), 297.

the public library system was engaged in a racializing project, one whose purpose was to inculcate European ethnics into whiteness."[12] Maria Accardi, as interviewed by Robert Schroeder in *Critical Journeys*, suggests that lack of theory in graduate library programs may be because "the goal was to prepare you to be a practitioner."[13] It is perhaps not unusual for LIS programs that offer the master's degree exclusively rather than master's and doctoral degrees to not offer many courses in theory, though I have heard and read about many librarians who wish they had the opportunity to take theory courses.[14]

Despite my lack of training in feminist theory during my formal education, many of my education and work experiences prior to becoming a librarian (and then a library director) were informed by feminist practice. Archaeology is a collaborative discipline; it is not possible to do the work alone. Fieldwork and lab work in college and graduate school with teams of people of a range of ages, experiences, and backgrounds, as well as working with my cohort of graduate students in our student association and as research assistants, all offered the opportunity to learn with and from others as we worked toward a shared goal. In my work in online publishing I was often a member of teams with little hierarchy and lots of opportunities for everyone to contribute. When I was hired into my first full-time library position to coordinate library instruction, I was accustomed to working as part of a team. Working as Instruction Coordinator with my library faculty colleagues, faculty in other departments, and students, where I was untenured and had the least seniority, both within the library and at the college, required much collaboration, and I continued to draw on feminist practice in that role.

By the time I applied for the position of library director, my prior experiences had given me a firm, if shallow, grounding in feminist practice, providing a base from which I could continue to learn about feminist theory and build my knowledge of intersectional feminism.

---

12 Todd Honma, "Trippin' Over the Color Line: The Invisibility of Race in Library and Information Studies," *InterActions: UCLA Journal of Education and Information Studies* 1, no. 2 (2005), 6.

13 Maria Accardi interviewed by Robert Schroeder, *Critical Journeys: How 14 Librarians Came to Embrace Critical Practice*, (Sacramento, CA: Library Juice Press, 2014), 8.

14 Ibid.

Bringing Feminism Into My Leadership Role

I would not have considered applying for a library director position if not for feminism. The statistics on diversity of all kinds in the library profession and among library leaders are disappointing, to say the least: 88% of librarians are white, as are 71% of students in MLIS programs.[15] Additionally, though 80% of all librarians identify as female, "only 58% of directors of ARL libraries are female."[16] Research by Christine L. Williams has shown that white, heterosexual men in feminized professions—of which librarianship is one—benefit from "the assumption that they are better suited than women for leadership positions."[17] And while many of the perceived attributes of management positions may discourage women and those in marginalized groups from seeking them out, as Chris Bourg has noted:

> If all of you who don't want to play politics, who don't want power
> & influence to change your values, and who want to have a healthy
> work life balance shy away from leadership positions; it might mean
> that you are leaving the leadership of our profession in the hands of
> those who aren't concerned about those things.[18]

When the former Library Director at City Tech announced his retirement in early 2014, I took seriously the disparity in men and women at the library director level. I applied for and accepted the position later that year.

My initial year as Chief Librarian was busy, with lots of change to manage both during and after the transition into my new role. During that time several library faculty and staff retired or moved to other positions, a few new staff positions were created and, as a

---

15 Chris Bourg, "Lack of Diversity By the Numbers in Librarianship and in Book
  Stuff," *Feral Librarian* (blog), February 22, 2014. https://chrisbourg.wordpress.
  com/2014/02/22/lack-of-diversity-by-the-numbers-in-librarianship-and-in-book-stuff/.

16 Ibid.

17 Christine L. Williams, "The Glass Escalator, Revisited: Gender Inequality in
  Neoliberal Times," *Gender & Society* 27, no. 5 (2013), 609.

18 Chris Bourg, "Mentors, Gender, Reluctance: Notes from Taiga Panel on
  Leadership at ER&L," *Feral Librarian* (blog), March 24, 2014. https://chrisbourg.
  wordpress.com/2014/03/24/mentors-gender-reluctance-notes-from-taiga-panel-on-
  leadership-at-erl/.

result of these changes, many library faculty and staff responsibilities were reorganized. My predecessor had modeled transparency in his leadership work, sharing information with us from the meetings he attended with the administration or of various college and university committees. During the time of transition I felt that transparency was essential, and I continue to share as much information as I can with library faculty and staff, both via email and in person. I am in full agreement with other feminist leaders who have emphasized the value of transparency; as Baharak Yousefi reminds us, "do not assume that you know what others need/don't need to know."[19]

With so many transitions in the library, I spent much of my first year and a half as director recruiting and hiring to fill newly vacant positions. Much has been published in recent years on the search and interview process in library hiring as part of the ever-increasing conversation on the lack of diversity in libraries. Fobazi Ettarh stresses the importance of intersectionality in the profession of librarianship, and the need for librarians "to educate ourselves on how these intersecting oppressions affect our community."[20] April Hathcock considers the librarian job search and finds that "an application process rooted in whiteness can have a chilling effect on the types of applicants who actually apply, creating a self-selection process that further promotes whiteness in the profession."[21] Angela Galvan addresses librarian job interviews and also finds that "the interview process is a series of repetitive gestures designed to mimic and reinforce white middle class values."[22] The work of these scholars was foremost in my mind as I strove for a feminist and anti-racist hiring practice.

---

19 Baharak Yousefi, "How to be a Good (Library) Boss," *Letters to a Young Librarian* (blog), May 19, 2016. https://letterstoayounglibrarian.blogspot.com/2016/05/how-to-be-good-library-boss-by-baharak.html.

20 Fobazi Ettarh, "Making a New Table: Intersectional Librarianship," *In the Library With the Lead Pipe*, July 2, 2014. http://www.inthelibrarywiththeleadpipe.org/2014/making-a-new-table-intersectional-librarianship-3/.

21 April Hathcock "White Librarianship in Blackface: Diversity Initiatives in LIS," *In the Library With the Lead Pipe*, October 7, 2015. http://www.inthelibrarywiththeleadpipe.org/2015/lis-diversity/.

22 Angela Galvan, "Soliciting Performance, Hiding Bias: Whiteness and Librarianship," *In the Library With the Lead Pipe*, June 3, 2015. http://www.inthelibrarywiththeleadpipe.org/2015/soliciting-performance-hiding-bias-whiteness-and-librarianship/.

I added our college's Equal Employment Opportunity statement at the beginning of each job ad we circulated, supplementing its usual appearance at the end of the ad. During search committee meetings we overtly discussed the diversity of the applicant pool for each position, in addition to considering the college-provided Affirmative Action statistics for the Library. These efforts are just a start; the next time we are able to hire I will continue to look for ways to increase the diversity of our applicant pool, including promoting positions via listservs and publications of the American Library Association ethnic caucuses.

I also bring feminism into my leadership practice by scheduling regular meetings with everyone who works in the library. While meetings are often reviled in libraries, academia, and other organizational settings for their potential to waste time, I appreciate meetings as a way to both discuss and work together towards shared goals, and I try to be mindful of others' time and commitments by planning (and following) an agenda. In my current role, this means regular meetings with all full-time library faculty and staff, both clerical and professional; with the library faculty and professional staff; and one-on-one meetings with each member of the library faculty and staff whom I supervise directly. Our all-library meeting is a dedicated time for us to share information with each other about regular library operations and projects. It is a useful opportunity for me as a leader and for all of our library workers—Public Services and Technical Services, faculty and staff—to stay informed about our experiences with our jobs and with members of the college community. I should note that at City Tech we have a relatively small library with a total of 24 full-time workers (myself included). I acknowledge that in a small library with a relatively flat hierarchy, transparency and communication via meetings and other means may be easier to implement than in a larger or multi-site library.

Continuing to Learn About Intersectional Feminism and Anti-Racism

As I have learned more about feminist theory, I have been led to the related themes of intersectionality, whiteness, and racism and continuing bias against marginalized peoples, and to striving for inclusive practice in my leadership work and beyond. The chapters on race and feminist class struggle in *Feminism Is For Everybody* were my introduction to intersectionality, after which I read legal scholar Kimberlé Crenshaw's 1989 article in which she coined the term. In her analysis of several anti-discrimination cases, Crenshaw demonstrated that the use of a "single-axis framework" to keep gender and race separate rendered the experiences of black women invisible.[23] Given the continued whiteness of librarianship, taking action to make my feminism intersectional seems especially critical, following Crenshaw's assertion that "feminism must include an analysis of race if it hopes to express the aspirations of non-white women."[24] As Crenshaw and Ortega have noted, working with and learning about women of color forces white women to acknowledge their participation in the system of white privilege, which is difficult,[25] a reality that I continue to face in my own studies.

I have made it a priority to learn more about intersectional feminism. Many of the professional development opportunities available to me enable intentional learning about feminism and anti-racism. At conferences, I seek out sessions on topics in critical librarianship and diversity and inclusion in higher education, and I have also participated in anti-racism workshops outside of librarianship. Some provide opportunities for white people to work specifically with other white people. They provide a place for white people to learn more about dismantling white supremacy without requesting that people of color, who experience racism every day, take on the additional work of educating us. Face to face and interpersonal venues for learning are valuable because they offer a chance to listen to and learn from others and to work through difficult topics together. I also appreciate that attending conferences and workshops can provide dedicated time and space for learning and reflection. While I am an introvert, I work to push past the hesitation I can feel at the prospect of engaging in difficult discussions. It is important to do this work in conversation with others, since sexism, racism, and other forms of oppression are structural, persistent problems without easy solutions.

---

23 Kimberlé Crenshaw, "Demarginalizing the Intersection of Race and Sex: A Black Feminist Critique of Antidiscrimination Doctrine, Feminist Theory, and Antiracist Politics," *University of Chicago Legal Forum* 1 (1989), 139-140.

24 Ibid.,166.

25 Ibid.,154; and FOrtega, "Being Lovingly, Knowingly Ignorant," 68.

I have also continued to engage in self-directed learning about feminism and anti-racism. There is so much to read, from academic books and articles to magazine and newspaper pieces, and I have also changed my fiction reading habits to regularly scan the #weneeddiversebooks[26] lists for leisure reading suggestions. I am grateful to librarians and others who have created reading lists and collected resources on these topics.[27] Twitter remains one of my favorite venues for self-directed learning. Even as the social media platform has changed over the years to become more overtly corporate, and despite very real concerns about the environment of toxic harassment that many women, people of color, those who identify as LGBTQ+, and other marginalized people face, Twitter still represents a unique opportunity to listen and learn. Listening is key: by respectfully listening and giving space for those who do not share our identit(ies) to engage in discussion, we can learn much about how we can all work to resist sexism, racism, and oppression in all forms. And as Elvia Arroyo-Ramirez and Jenna Freedman emphasized in their workshop on microagressions and zines at the LACUNY Institute in 2016, zines (and other media) produced by people of color are a terrific way for whites to self-educate without burdening people of color.[28]

Continued learning has made me more aware of the lack of intersectional feminist perspectives in events, programs, and conversations across my work in academic librarianship and as a library director. Two decades ago, Jane Anne Hannigan and Hilary Crew emphasized the need to question male-focused management models in LIS education, and wondered how librarianship "can resist the domination of male management models that encompass gender/power inequalities in their basic assumptions, especially when such inequalities are embedded in the rhetoric of texts used

---

26 *We Need Diverse Books*, accessed August 13, 2016, http://weneeddiversebooks.org/.

27 Hathcock, "Recommended Reading," *At the Intersection*; Jessica Schomburg, "#CritLib and Diversity Related Books that I've Read," *Research about Cataloging and Assessment and More...* https://catassessmentresearch.blogspot.com/2016/02/critlib-and-diversity-related-books.html.

28 Elvia Arroyo-Ramirez and Jenna Freedman, "Offensive Mechanisms, Constructive Paths: How to Recognize and Deal with Microaggressions in the LIS Field" (presentation at the LACUNY Institute, Race Matters: Libraries, Racism, and Antiracism, Brooklyn, NY, June 2016).

in the educational process."[29] Beyond LIS graduate coursework there are many professional programs that focus on library leadership, in academic and other libraries, which often aim to develop management skills among librarians who are interested in leadership or who may have come into a leadership position without explicit training. However, as Jessica Olin and Michelle Millet have shared about their experiences "gender is barely mentioned, if at all, in such settings."[30] While I have found much of value in my own experiences with leadership development, I have found the lack of explicitly feminist and intersectional teachings on leadership to be all the more stark given the diversity expressed by my fellow attendees of these programs.

Though I did not learn more about intersectional feminism early in my education and careers, one advantage of my delay is that I have immediate contexts in which to apply theory to practice in my work. Scholars including Maria Accardi, Jane Anne Hannigan, and Jennifer Vinopal have offered concrete suggestions for feminist library leadership practice.[31] In the process of hiring several tenure-track library faculty, I have and continue to be mindful of not just recruitment, but also retention. Research has shown that the promotion and tenure process can be especially fraught for women, people of color, and other marginalized groups, both in academic libraries and academia more generally.[32] Karin Griffin notes that many of the usual tensions in the relationships between librarians and faculty "can exacerbate a sense of exclusion" for people of

---

29 Jane Anne Hannigan and Hilary Crew, "A Feminist Paradigm for Library and Information Science," *Wilson Library Bulletin* 68, no. 2 (1993), 29.

30 Jessica Olin and Michelle Millet, "Gendered Expectations for Leadership in Libraries," *In the Library With the Lead Pipe*, November 4, 2015. http://www. inthelibrarywiththeleadpipe.org/2015/libleadgender/.

31 Hannigan, "A Feminist Standpoint;" Accardi, *Feminist Pedagogy for Library Instruction*; Jennifer Vinopal "The Quest for Diversity in Library Staffing: From Awareness to Action," *In the Library With the Lead Pipe,* January 13, 2016. http:// www.inthelibrarywiththeleadpipe.org/2016/quest-for-diversity/.

32 Ione T. Damasco and Dracine Hodges, "Tenure and Promotion Experiences of Academic Librarians of Color," *College & Research Libraries* 73, no. 3 (2012): 279-301; and Tricia Matthew, "Here on the Margins: My Academic Home," *PMLA* 130, no. 5 (2015): 1510-1514.

color.[33] In their panel at the Association of College and Research Libraries Conference, Jaena Alabi, Bridget Farrell, Claudine Jenda, and Pambanisha Whaley discussed the importance of inclusivity in the library workplace, and shared details both on what to watch for—microaggressions, imposter syndrome, and burnout —and the value of mentoring.[34]

I appreciate the opportunity to learn more about intersectional feminism and to feed theory back into my practice. I may have come to theory late, but it is still very much of value to me as a library leader, for as Accardi notes in *Critical Journeys*: "you can practice feminist pedagogy without understanding or being aware of the theory, but in order for it to really transform you as a teacher, you need to know the theories or be aware of them."[35]

Embracing the Novice Mindset: Challenges and Opportunities

While I embrace the novice mindset and commit myself to continual learning, striving for intersectional feminist library leadership is not without challenges for me. Time is paramount: I must intentionally make time for this work though time can be in short supply as a director. I am not alone in this concern, as Jennifer Vinopal has asked: "How can leaders maintain a focus on these issues and hold themselves and the organization accountable, even while tending to all the other work of the organization?" I appreciate the suggestions that she offers in her article for actionable ways forward, which include recommendations for creating a diversity plan, recruitment, mentoring, and internships.[36]

The process of submitting a proposal for and then writing this essay has led me to read more, and to read with more purpose. And

---

33 Karin Griffin, "Pursuing Tenure and Promotion in the Academy: A Librarian's Cautionary Tale," *Negro Educational Review* 64, no. 1-4 (2013): 95.

34 Jaena Alabi, Bridget Farrell, Claudine Jenda, and Pambanisha Whaley, "You Belong Here: The Importance of Cultivating an Inclusive Organizational Culture" (presentation, Association of College and Research Libraries Conference, Portland, OR, March 25-28, 2015).

35 Accardi, Schroeder, *Critical Journeys*, 12.

36 Vinopal, "The Quest for Diversity."

as I read and learn more I also wrestle with impostor syndrome, as I know others do. Have I missed out on too much by not studying feminist theory in college or graduate school? Have I learned enough—and have I put my new knowledge into practice enough—to call myself a feminist leader? Will I ever? I have worked with and through these feelings as I write this essay, uncertain that I have read enough to begin writing, an exercise in the discomfort of questioning what I know. I have pushed past this discomfort enough to get to this point, to a finished essay, and to an uneasy truce with the feeling that there will never be a finished state to this project, to research and learning about intersectional feminism. The work is ongoing, as much important work is, and I must embrace that if I am truly committed to the goal to "take every opportunity possible to interrogate the very systems and structures that gave you the aforementioned seat at the table."[37]

Much of what I have learned through my reading and professional development—both in library contexts and more broadly—has been directly relevant to my work as a library director, though finding ways to bring intersectional feminism to my work more overtly can be difficult. While many libraries have convened discussion groups or committees to read and learn about diversity and inclusion, as Bourg has noted, requiring library workers to attend a program, join a committee, or complete a shared reading does not feel like a feminist act.[38] I have also been concerned that an open invitation to participate may lead those who choose not to participate to be perceived negatively. However, as Annie Pho and Turner Masland have suggested, "we are now at a point where discussions about the intersectionality of gender, sexuality, race, and ethnicity in librarianship are happening among a wider audience,"[39] which can lead us to initial conversations in our workplace. As well, Juleah Swanson, Ione Damasco, Isabel Gonzalez-Smith, Dracine Hodges, Todd Honma, and Azusa Tanaka remind us

---

37 Yousefi, "How to be a Good (Library) Boss."

38 Chris Bourg, "The Radicalism Is Coming from Inside the Library," *Feral Librarian* (blog), December 10, 2015. https://chrisbourg.wordpress.com/2015/12/10/the-radicalism-is-coming-from-inside-the-library/.

39 Annie Pho and Turner Masland, "The Revolution Will Not Be Stereotyped: Changing Perceptions through Diversity," in *The Librarian Stereotype: Deconstructing Perceptions and Presentations of Information Work*, ed. by Nicole Pagowsky and Miriam Rigby (Chicago, IL: Association of College & Research Libraries, 2015), 277.

that a focus on the reality of structural and institutional sexism, racism, and other discrimination may make it easier to discuss diversity and inclusion at work, and focus on what we as members of the organization can do to address these issues.[40]

As a white woman in a leadership position at a large, public, commuter college that enrolls a student population that is racially, ethnically, and economically diverse, I must also be mindful of the lure of white guilt and the white savior complex. The overt focus on social justice is one aspect of City Tech and CUNY that I admire and find meaningful. However, as Gina Schesselman-Tarango notes in her analysis of feminism and white supremacy in libraries, white women especially must be careful not to "conceive of those who benefit from our services—in particular, those who have historically been or are presently 'Othered'—as less-than, deficient, inherently needy, or in need of 'saving'."[41] Similarly, though it is easy to feel guilty about the ways in which I benefit from white privilege and white feminism, guilt is not productive. I have started with self-education and am not finished, and I must continue to look for opportunities to help dismantle systemic sexism, racism, and other forms of discrimination.

Acknowledging and accepting that I will make mistakes as I work to incorporate intersectional feminism into my leadership practice is another challenge. I have made mistakes in the past and will certainly make them in the future, and it is important that I own and learn from them. Sometimes it means coming to recognize the difference between intent and impact, and other times it is realizing that I missed a chance to do or say something to disrupt the predominant discriminatory narrative, and vowing to do better in the future. The novice mindset can be valuable and push us to learn, but it is ultimately a vulnerable position, and it can be uncomfortable when asking questions reveals gaps in our knowledge. I acknowledge, too, that as a leader I am in a position of power and it is in many ways easier for me to make mistakes, though I also understand that if I

---

40 Juleah Swanson, Ione Damasco, Isabel Gonzalez-Smith, Dracine Hodges, Todd Honma and Azusa Tanaka, "Why Diversity Matters: A Roundtable Discussion on Racial and Ethnic Diversity in Librarianship," *In the Library With the Lead Pipe,* July 29, 2015. http://www.inthelibrarywiththeleadpipe.org/2015/why-diversity-matters-a-roundtable-discussion-on-racial-and-ethnic-diversity-in-librarianship/.

41 Gina Schlesselman-Tarango, "The Legacy of Lady Bountiful: White Women in the Library," *Library Trends* 64, no. 4 (2016): 681.

make too many mistakes I risk losing trust. I work to remind myself that my vulnerability and occasional discomfort makes me a better leader and helps to foster a workplace environment that supports asking questions, making mistakes, learning, and growing. Further, I am cheered by the assertion by James Williams III and Jolanda-Pieta van Arnhem that "every interaction matters;" every day I have the opportunity to intentionally bring intersectional feminism to my practice.[42]

My travels on the road to feminist library leadership are not complete, and I take comfort in hooks' words when she reminds us that "There is no path to feminism."[43] I hope that in sharing my winding and ongoing journey I can encourage others, whatever your stage of education or career or your aspirations towards leadership, to embrace the novice mindset and learn more about intersectional feminism. For me it is a worthwhile goal: working to help build the intersectional feminist library future I want to be a part of.

---

42 James Williams III and Jolanda-Pieta van Arnhem, "But Then You Have to Make It Happen," *Code4Lib Journal* 28 (2015).

43 hooks, *Feminism Is For Everybody*, 116.

Selected Learning Resources

In addition to the articles, books, and websites cited above, I have found these resources useful in learning more about intersectional feminism, anti-racism, and resisting the oppression of marginalized people:

- The University of Minnesota Gender, Women & Sexuality Studies program has created downloadable online modules to provide an introduction to many of the topics covered in their courses: Empire, The Gaze, Gender, Intersectionality, and Whiteness.

  http://cla.umn.edu/gwss/research/digital-humanities-social-justice/elearning-modules

- Hunter College, CUNY Sociology professor Jessie Daniels studies racism and feminism; the series "Trouble with White Feminists" on the Racism Review blog collects her posts that explore white feminism specifically.

  http://www.racismreview.com/blog/2015/12/30/review-trouble-with-white-feminism/

- The critlib community of librarians interested in critical librarianship also maintains a website with information about the regular #critlib Twitter chats, upcoming and past unconferences and symposia, and recommended readings.

  http://critlib.org

- The Everyday Feminism website features articles and comics written for a general audience on feminism, anti-racism, and anti-LBGTQ+ discrimination.

  http://everydayfeminism.com/

Bibliography

Accardi, Maria T. *Feminist Pedagogy for Library Instruction.* Sacramento, CA: Library Juice Press, 2013.

Accardi, Maria and Robert Schroeder. *Critical Journeys: How 14 Librarians Came to Embrace Critical Practice.* Sacramento, CA: Library Juice Press, 2014.

Alabi, Jaena, Bridget Farrell, Claudine Jenda, and Pambanisha Whaley. "You Belong Here: The Importance of Cultivating an Inclusive Organizational Culture." Presentation at the Association of College and Research Libraries Conference, Portland, OR, March 25-28, 2015.

Arroyo-Ramirez, Elvia, and Jenna Freedman. "Offensive Mechanisms, Constructive Paths: How to Recognize and Deal with Microaggressions in the LIS Field." Presentation at the LACUNY Institute, Race Matters: Libraries, Racism, and Antiracism, Brooklyn, NY, May 20, 2016.

Bourg, Chris. "The Radicalism Is Coming from Inside the Library." *Feral Librarian* (blog). December 10, 2015. https://chrisbourg. wordpress.com/2015/12/10/the-radicalism-is-coming-from-inside-the-library/.

———— "Mentors, Gender, Reluctance: Notes from Taiga Panel on Leadership at ER&L." *Feral Librarian* (blog). March 24, 2014. https://chrisbourg.wordpress.com/2014/03/24/mentors-gender-reluctance-notes-from-taiga-panel-on-leadership-at-erl/.

———— "Lack of Diversity By the Numbers in Librarianship and in Book Stuff." *Feral Librarian* (blog). February 22, 2014. https://chrisbourg.wordpress.com/2014/02/22/lack-of-diversity-by-the-numbers-in-librarianship-and-in-book-stuff/.

City University of New York. "Mission & History." Accessed August 13, 2016. http://www2.cuny.edu/about/history.

Crenshaw, Kimberlé. "Demarginalizing the Intersection of Race and Sex: A Black Feminist Critique of Antidiscrimination Doctrine, Feminist Theory, and Antiracist Politics." *University of Chicago Legal Forum* 1 (1989): 139-167.

"Critlib Twitter Chats." Accessed August 13, 2016. http://critlib.org/twitter-chats.

Damasco, Ione T., and Dracine Hodges. "Tenure and Promotion Experiences of Academic Librarians of Color." *College & Research Libraries* 73, no. 3 (2012): 279-301.

Elmborg, James. "Critical Information Literacy: Implications for Instructional Practice." *The Journal of Academic Librarianship* 32, no. 2 (2006): 192-199.

Ettarh, Fobazi. "Making a New Table: Intersectional Librarianship." *In the Library With the Lead Pipe.* July 2, 2014. http://www.inthelibrarywiththeleadpipe.org/2014/making-a-new-table-intersectional-librarianship-3/.

Freire, Paulo. *Pedagogy of the Oppressed,* 30th anniversary ed. New York: Continuum, 2000.

Galvan, Angela. "Soliciting Performance, Hiding Bias: Whiteness and Librarianship." *In the Library With the Lead Pipe.* June 3, 2015. http://www.inthelibrarywiththeleadpipe.org/2015/soliciting-performance-hiding-bias-whiteness-and-librarianship/.

Griffin, Karin. "Pursuing Tenure and Promotion in the Academy: A Librarian's Cautionary Tale." *Negro Educational Review* 64, no. 1-4 (2013): 77-96.

Hannigan, Jane Anne. "A Feminist Standpoint for Library and Information Science Education." *Journal of Education for Library and Information Science* 35, no. 4 (1994): 297-319.

Hannigan, Jane Anne, and Hilary Crew. "A Feminist Paradigm for Library and Information Science." *Wilson Library Bulletin* 68, no. 2 (1993): 28-32.

Hathcock, April. "Recommended Reading." *At the Intersection.* Accessed August 13, 2016, https://aprilhathcock.wordpress.com/recommended-reading/.

———— "White Librarianship in Blackface: Diversity Initiatives in LIS." *In the Library With the Lead Pipe.* October 7, 2015. http://www.inthelibrarywiththeleadpipe.org/2015/lis-diversity/.

Holschuh-Simmons, Michelle. "Librarians As Disciplinary Discourse Mediators: Using Genre Theory to Move Toward Critical Information Literacy." *portal: Libraries & the Academy* 5, no. 3 (2005): 297-311.

Honma, Todd. "Trippin' Over the Color Line: The Invisibility of Race in Library and Information Studies." *InterActions: UCLA Journal of Education and Information Studies* 1, no. 2 (2005): 1-26.

hooks, bell. *Feminism Is for Everybody.* Cambridge, MA: South End Press, 2000.

Leonard, Anne, and Maura A. Smale. "The Three Credit Solution: Social Justice in an Information Literacy Course." In *Information Literacy and Social Justice*, edited by Lua Gregory and Shana Higgins, 143-161. Sacramento, CA: Library Juice Press, 2013.

Matthew, Tricia. "Here on the Margins: My Academic Home." *PMLA* 130, no. 5 (2015): 1510-1514.

Olin, Jessica, and Michelle Millet. "Gendered Expectations for Leadership in Libraries." *In the Library With the Lead Pipe.* November 4, 2015. http://www.inthelibrarywiththeleadpipe. org/2015/libleadgender/.

Ortega, Mariana. "Being Lovingly, Knowingly Ignorant: White Feminism and Women of Color." *Hypatia* 21, no. 3 (2006): 56-74.

Pho, Annie, and Turner Masland. "The Revolution Will Not Be Stereotyped: Changing Perceptions through Diversity." In *The Librarian Stereotype: Deconstructing Perceptions and Presentations of Information Work*, edited by Nicole Pagowsky and Miriam Rigby, 257-282. Chicago, IL: Association of College & Research Libraries, 2015.

Schlesselman-Tarango, Gina. "The Legacy of Lady Bountiful: White Women in the Library." *Library Trends* 64, no. 4 (2016): 667-686.

Schomburg, Jessica. "#CritLib and Diversity Related Books that I've Read," *Research about Cataloging and Assessment and More...*, Accessed August 14, 2016. https://catassessmentresearch.blogspot. com/2016/02/critlib-and-diversity-related-books.html.

Smale, Maura A. "Beyond Livetweeting: Twitter Chats for Professional Development." *ACRLog* (blog). April 21, 2014. http://acrlog.org/2014/04/21/beyond-livetweeting-twitter-chats-for-professional-development.

Swanson, Juleah, Ione Damasco, Isabel Gonzalez-Smith, Dracine Hodges, Todd Honma, and Azusa Tanaka. "Why Diversity Matters: A Roundtable Discussion on Racial and Ethnic Diversity in Librarianship." *In the Library With the Lead Pipe*. July 29, 2015. http://www.inthelibrarywiththeleadpipe.org/2015/why-diversity-matters-a-roundtable-discussion-on-racial-and-ethnic-diversity-in-librarianship/.

We Need Diverse Books. Accessed August 13, 2016. http://weneeddiversebooks.org/.

Williams, Christine L. "The Glass Escalator, Revisited: Gender Inequality in Neoliberal Times." *Gender & Society* 27, no. 5 (2013): 609-629.

Williams III, James, and Jolanda-Pieta van Arnhem. "But Then You Have to Make It Happen." *Code4Lib Journal* 28 (2015): http://journal.code4lib.org/articles/10487.

Vinopal, Jennifer. "The Quest for Diversity in Library Staffing: From Awareness to Action." *In the Library With the Lead Pipe*. January 13, 2016. http://www.inthelibrarywiththeleadpipe.org/2016/quest-for-diversity/.

Yousefi, Baharak. "How to be a Good (Library) Boss." *Letters to a Young Librarian* (blog). May 19, 2016. https://letterstoayounglibrarian.blogspot.com/2016/05/how-to-be-good-library-boss-by-baharak.html.

CREATING A PATH TO FEMINIST LEADERSHIP

Shirley Lew

I am currently the dean of the library at a community college. I'm a feminist and I apply feminist praxis in my role as a leader, particularly critical feminist pedagogy.

These statements are true, yet they feel false or at least portray an incomplete picture, as my path to both leadership and feminism was indirect and unplanned. Truer statements would be that I became a leader by circumstance, and that my feminist consciousness evolved over time, and came into clearer focus with each leadership role I took on. As bell hooks says, "[t]here is no one path to feminism".[1] In this chapter, I will explore, using personal narrative, my path to feminist leadership and address some basic questions I think about every day: What does feminist leadership mean to me? How do I put into practice a feminist leadership in libraries? What does a library run on feminist principles look like?

My approach in this discussion draws upon feminist inquiry and feminist epistemology. In delving into my own story, I take encouragement from the feminist principles that "the personal transforms into the political" and "concrete lived experience is a key place from which to build knowledge and foment social change".[2]

---

1 bell hooks, *Feminism is for Everybody: Passionate Politics* (Cambridge: South End Press, 2000), 116.

2 Sharlene Nagy Hesse-Biber, "Feminist Research: Exploring, Interrogating, and Transforming the Interconnections of Epistemology, Methodology, and Method" in *Handbook of Feminist Research: Theory and Praxis*, ed. Sharlene Nagy Hesse-Biber (Los Angeles: Sage Publications, 2012), 2.

Further, as a woman of colour practicing in a field long dominated by whiteness, I draw from Paulo Freire's writings about systems of oppression, and the critical reflection that the oppressed use to raise consciousness and inform action. Freire's call for a transformative praxis based on reflection and action is central to my practice.[3] This chapter is part of that process of reflection and considers how I can bring about change as a leader.

I am not a feminist scholar (I'm actively learning) but I know enough to understand the need for someone like me to speak personally, and therefore politically. Nevertheless, the self-doubt remains as I worry whether I have anything useful to say. There is anxiety as well, about taking up space and time with what feels like navel-gazing. Erin Wunker describes my feelings perfectly when she says, in the introduction to *Notes from a Feminist Killjoy*, "Who do I think I am?" Wunker describes the crisis she felt writing in the first person, and how vulnerable she felt using the pronoun "I", a response she intellectually understood is rooted in patriarchal ideas of the "I" connoting the confessional, or a feminized type of writing.[4] She concludes:

> [T]he personal pronoun *I* is crucial; it's a site from which we can take stock, take responsibility, and take space if space is needed… Situating yourself enacts the deliberate practice of locating your own identity and experiences as coming from somewhere and being mediated by certain things such as your race, gender, and class. Laying these things out for yourself locates your way of being in the world—your knowledge—within larger systems of knowing.[5]

Her declaration is true and it's helpful. It's also helpful for me to view the writing of this essay as taking steps "from the margin to the center" as bell hooks urges us to do, despite how uncomfortable it is to move away from the familiar. The writing feels risky, but necessary, as Wunker says, to situate myself as a library leader.

In terms of locating my identity, I offer a few facts about myself. I'm a cisgender, heterosexual, first-generation Chinese-Canadian. I

---

3 Paulo Freire, *Pedagogy of the Oppressed*, 30th anniversary ed. (New York: Continuum International, 2001), 14.

4 Erin Wunker, *Notes from a Feminist Killjoy: Essays on Everyday Life* (Toronto: BookThug, 2016), 11.

5 Ibid., 30-31.

am not fluent in speaking or reading Chinese, although I look as if I should be, which has caused problems. In language and culture I relate more strongly with western society, although it's my Chinese roots that have most sharply and, at times, painfully defined my identity and sense of (non)belonging. The ways in which I am privileged are many. I'm presently in a named position of power that gives me the space to be transparent and vulnerable, with low risk. I have job security, benefits, and a salary well above average. I am able bodied and neuronormative. I am well loved and supported by my partner, my friends, and my family.

There are aspects of my identity and present reality that aren't as neatly described and are perhaps best understood as oppositional. I know what systemic racism, injustice, intolerance, and invisibility feel like, and I am also at the center of a post-secondary system that has traditionally oppressed those with less power. I come from a family and a culture characterized by quiet acceptance, even when confronted with hate, and yet I am in a position in my work and community that requires that I speak out loudly and often, and act decisively. Growing up, I so internalized my marginalization, that what caught my imagination wasn't the stories of the Chinese people in Canada, but rather the white stories I found in novels and history books. These white stories seemed to me to hold the key to understanding and accessing the "real" world, whereas the actual world I was in felt unreal or not important. Most difficult to admit was the extent to which I rejected the language and culture of my family. In an act of self-marginalization, as early as five years old I refused to speak the rural Chinese dialect of my parents. At five, I was exposed to school, and the experience confirmed what I had already intuited: the language of my home life was best kept hidden indoors as it had no value or currency in the outside world. There were clear signs that even the dialect we spoke exposed us and made us vulnerable. When receiving guests or interacting with anyone in a public sphere, my parents switched from Toisanese, a dialect of Chinese hillbillies, to Cantonese, a dialect of urbane Hong Kong. The double whammy of the wrong language and the wrong dialect explained the barriers to opportunity that I could see my parents struggling against, and by extension, the difficulty they had in extending opportunities to their children. To this day, I can't speak any dialect of Chinese, and rejecting the language had, at the time, the desired effect of providing a type of entry into the dominant society. Even as I can reflect on, and understand, the multi-layered reasons for my self-oppression as a young child, the emotions it conjures—anger, shame, powerlessness—are raw. These conflicting elements are very active components of my identity and inform the way I understand myself in my current role. I know that I never want to experience that level of shame or powerlessness again, and that these emotions, regardless of how neatly compartmentalized and deeply buried, are fundamental to who I am. Similarly, my sensitivity to power and oppression, and how they are embedded in systems of language and culture, is finely tuned from these life experiences. I share these details not because I think they're particularly unusual, but because it's important to provide a context for a feminist leadership coming from a place of intersectional marginalization. I know I bring a different and much-needed perspective on what social justice, equity, and inclusion can be like for students and staff at a public educational institution. At the same time, I also know that my underlying emotions can be easily triggered and cause a gut reaction to issues, as opposed to one that creates a better chance for real change. The emotional is personal is political.

In discussing my path to becoming a library leader, and my feelings about having this role in this community, it's relevant to mention how I got my first professional position as a librarian. Fresh out of library school in 1999, I was offered a full-time position in a web and technology role, areas I intentionally focused on in school and had a strong interest in. A week into my new job, it became evident that a key reason I was offered the position was because I was mistaken for the other Asian woman in my graduating class (there were only two of us), the other woman having made a strong impression on my boss in a course in which my boss was lecturing. I never took that course. The Other Asian Woman had a completely different set of skills and professional interests than I did. It need not be said, but it needs to be said: we did not look anything alike. The instructive element in this introduction to the library profession was not suddenly realizing that clumsy racism exists even in libraries, but that in the awkward moment when the two of us realized the mistaken identity, I immediately made light of it and labored to rectify the situation for my boss' sake. The retreat into silence and quiet acceptance is a hard habit to shake. These moments have played out repeatedly over the seventeen years I have been a librarian, the most recent occurring at my workplace after I had become the library director. Again, I was mistaken for the Other Asian Woman in a room of academic leaders where there were only two of us present. Being reminded of your invisibility is a powerful force of oppression and persists even with the right credentials or a named position of power.

After that first professional job, the positions I held were not a linear progression up a career ladder. It was more of a meander, taking opportunities as they arose, pursuing side projects that advanced issues or outcomes I believed in, seeking ways to work with people I respected inside and outside my organization. I was constructing my own professional sphere and community, one that made sense to me and one in which I felt I belonged, even if that sense of belonging was in a community of my own making and not recognized or sanctioned by the mainstream profession. I was in the system, doing rewarding and productive work, yet never quite shedding that cloak of invisibility. Why risk the embarrassment of assuming others saw me, when they didn't? In reality, many library people did see me, and encouraged and supported me, but trapped in the psychological space of feeling dominated, I felt their approval was not only unearned but also unreliable. From operating in this mode and mindset for many years, to then becoming a Director, then Dean, of the library was certainly not planned. A temporary acting appointment became permanent, and was then expanded, all in a period of sixteen months. While I went into these positions fully aware of their requirements and didn't question my ability to do them, the emotional transition to fully embodying leadership was a longer journey. To practice leadership with honesty and authenticity, I had to discard the cloak of invisibility. However, rather than feeling seen, I felt utterly exposed, and I was not prepared for it.

Unpacking that feeling of exposure at the very moment the establishment had validated me and handed me significant power created a small crisis. Freire provides some insight:

> The oppressed, having internalized the image of the oppressor and adopted his guidelines, are fearful of freedom... without freedom, [the oppressed] cannot exist authentically... They are at one and the same time themselves and the oppressor whose consciousness they have internalized. The conflict lies in the choice between being wholly themselves or being divided; between ejecting the oppressor

within or not ejecting them; between human solidarity or alienation; between following prescriptions or having choices; between being spectators or actors; between acting or having the illusion of acting through the action of the oppressors; between speaking out or being silent, castrated in their power to create and recreate, in their power to transform the world.[6]

Leaving aside Freire's dated and problematic implication that the oppressed and oppressors are all male, his words nevertheless came as a surprise. I thought I was self-aware and had done the work of understanding the impact of racism and marginalization. But Freire's call to exist authentically through the act of freeing oneself from oppressive systems hit me at the right time, and allowed me to really see and to feel the full weight of the oppression that I had willingly dragged along with me my entire life. I still had baggage, and this was a problem if I was going to be the kind of feminist leader I wanted to be. How could I ensure everyone in my library had a voice if I continued to silence myself? How could I advocate for real change in any context if I moved through the world being invisible when it suited me or when it was a convenient escape? Did I even know how to assert my presence without apology and without concerning myself with others' discomfort? Could I deal with other people's disappointment when they realize who I am, and not the person they thought or wished I was?

This baggage stemmed from my relationship with power and an uncomfortable history of acquiescing to it, giving it away like a hot potato whenever it was handed to me, and basically treating it as undesirable. To me, power was the force that oppressed and I was much more comfortable on the other side of it, resisting and working around it. I wasn't used to thinking about power in a context that wasn't negatively framed by patriarchy and colonialism and by inequity and injustice. I hadn't tried to imagine power in a feminist framework because I never got past the issue of whether feminism and institutional power were inherently contradictory systems. However, the day-to-day reality of my job brought me down to earth quickly. I had to reconcile my relationship with power if I was to achieve the freedom that Freire describes. I needed to be authentically and wholly myself if I was going to be a leader who was transparent, inclusive,

---

6 Freire, *Pedagogy of the Oppressed*, 47-48.

grounded in my values, and able to create the kind of safe environment I wanted for staff and students in the library. I also had to address the fact that practicing feminist leadership within a traditional institution was in some ways incongruent, and navigating those tensions would require an even greater level of transparency and also compromise.

The feeling of exposure I felt when placed in a leadership role begins to make more sense in the context of a lifetime of existing in the margins and having no apparatus to lean upon when placed at the center. This role challenged my unresolved issues with oppression and, even more problematic, with my self-oppression through self-censoring of language, culture, and my own voice at the very moments I needed to speak up. This realization was the necessary starting point for constructing a way toward a feminist leadership that could really enact change. I needed to accept and validate my experience as something real, and therefore common, and to start talking about it openly with those in my community and especially with other librarians of color. I needed to figure out how to use my experience to become better attuned to the ways in which our profession and workplaces continue to oppress, and yet not center these issues on me, and on my emotional triggers. I needed an apparatus, and visualizing what this might look like was key to a way forward. I imagined a physical support structure that was both an extension of me, yet separate. I envisioned a personal feminist framework that conformed to the shape of my body and experience, an exoskeleton of sorts, which acted as a filter for things coming in and going out. I visualize the framework as multilayered, at its foundation a perspective constructed from personal experience, and interwoven with the many books, feminist theories, and people in my community—friends, mentors, colleagues—who shape my thinking and values. The framework isn't static but rather it expands, contracts, and changes shape with time and experience. Visualizing this personal feminist framework works for me and is a way of carrying my community with me. It gives me a space to think objectively through a feminist lens, to add to and build upon theory and ideas, to learn and unlearn things as I encounter new situations. It's a filter through which I can separate the self from what's required in the moment, holding me accountable before I veer along the wrong path.

How does this framework operate in practice? On a day-to-day basis, it underlies everything from dealing with difficult emails, to writing policy, to navigating the power dynamics and politics in a meeting. For example, it helps me respond effectively to a group email thread where no consensus is being reached and discussion has stalled. The reflexive response is to intervene with an email suggesting a way forward and a possible solution. However, considered through a feminist lens, intervening in this way raises immediate questions. Is "suggesting a way forward" just a euphemistic way of stating what is really happening: I am using my position of power to impose a solution and thus quickly resolve the issue to the satisfaction (usually) of the most vocal among the group. The feminist framework encourages me to ask what is being overlooked in the name of convenience and efficiency. Whose views were once again in the minority or who had not spoken up at all? Is there a pattern of dominant voices overriding others under the guise of collaborative decision-making that needs to be called out? The right response is rarely the easy response, one that requires the deeper work necessary to truly address issues. Where the feminist framework is most required is in these moments of failure. It keeps me of aware of when I am taking the shortcut and reminds me that deeper issues ultimately cannot be ignored.

On a more macro-level, a feminist framework helps make sense of issues in the profession as a whole and in the academic library community specifically. At this level the issues are many: inaction regarding the lack of meaningful diversity in libraries; the need to engage with online privacy and surveillance issues, technically and politically; passive acceptance of licensing terms and exorbitant fees charged by academic publishers and content aggregators; allocation of our limited budgets to for-profit library software vendors despite reduction of choice and increasing costs; inability to reach a critical mass of support for open access and open source software which would allow us to collectively take control of our information and automation, and have these systems accessible by all institutions. On the surface, it's easy to point to the hypocrisy of our profession when it comes to declaring our values versus what we actually do. We espouse diversity but the profession remains overwhelmingly white. We purport to care about privacy and stewardship of our data, yet we turn our information over to closed proprietary systems, thereby forfeiting control without fully understanding the technology behind it. We fight for intellectual freedom, yet we allow our collections to shrink in scope and depth in order to purchase content from the same major academic publishers who dominate the market. We decry the profit-driven motives of software vendors, yet we continue to give them our business. We're unified in our support for equal access and level playing fields, yet the reality is a growing divide between big and small institutions due to divergent levels of commitment to consortial and cooperative approaches to technology and content. Of course, it's not as simple as hypocrisy—there are financial and political pressures that impact decisions made by all libraries. But viewed from a feminist perspective, the decision-making process as a whole is one fraught with issues of power, and driven by a culture and system that protects the status quo. We are less than forthright about these boundaries and hierarchies we have established in the library world based on sector, institution type, size, and urban versus rural geographic divisions: there are the systems at the center and the systems in the margin and a culture that maintains this order. It's a culture that designates power to a select few who set our priorities, who define what is acceptable practice, and who manage away voices of dissent or alternative approaches.

What is the feminist leadership response in this larger context? The feminist framework can provide perspective and help us recognize how even well-meaning organizations such as libraries can still create systems of oppression that marginalize, exclude, and consolidate power. The collective response from the library community has been largely silence. Drawing upon my experience of self-oppression, I find it unsettling to recognize the extent to which our female-dominant profession is actually patriarchal. bell hooks' observation that most women, and white feminists specifically, "have not decolonized their thinking"[7] feels relevant. She goes on to say:

> Since unenlightened white feminists were unwilling to acknowledge the spheres of American life where they acted and act in collusion with imperialist white supremacist capitalist patriarchy, sustained protest and resistance on the part of black women / women of color and our radical white sisters was needed to break the wall of denial.[8]

The paradox of feminists who collude with the patriarchy is like the paradox of librarians who enable systems of inaccessibility and

---

7 hooks, *Feminism is for Everybody*, 45.

8 Ibid., 46.

inequity. What is the feminist leadership response? How do we break the wall of denial? I return to Freire's theory of transformation through critical reflection and action. In many ways, we are doing the work of critical reflection and action with initiatives like the #critlib discussions taking place in Twitter, code of conduct policies at our conferences, increasing awareness of who we ask to speak to our communities as keynotes and panelists, and a growing body of writing about resistance within libraries.[9] A feminist leadership response expands these discussions to decision-making tables and does not remain silent. It starts by asking the questions that aren't being asked, raising issues that aren't part of the usual discourse, and suggesting changes to our processes to make them more inclusive and transparent. Feminism demands that we ask the questions and make the changes to ensure we are doing the things we say we are doing.

Described in this way, feminist leadership sounds bold, fearless, and uncompromising. And in many ways it is: feminist leadership forces the organization to slow down, to take the harder route, and to work for outcomes that may not be measurable within a timeframe that advances the short-term goals of organizations or careers. However, in those moments when there is an opportunity to enact change, what I still think about first is whether it is safe to speak up. I'm looking for my allies. I'm assessing the faces of those who have the most power in the room and I'm gauging the level of receptiveness. I may speak or just as likely I may decide to say nothing at all and wait. When I think about what a library run on feminist principles looks like, it's important that it look and feel different than it currently does. There don't have to be personal consequences for offering a different perspective or way of doing things. We can strive for a culture that says of itself: we have the resilience and capacity to take in and consider new ideas and to recognize when it is time to make bold changes. It is possible to create a safe environment for library workers and students to talk with one another about their concerns and needs without fear

---

9 For example, books published by Library Juice Press; open access journals *In the Library With a Lead Pipe* and *Journal of Critical Library and Information Studies*; the blogs and writings of April Hathcock (https://aprilhathcock.wordpress.com/), Chris Bourg (https://chrisbourg.wordpress.com/), Emily Drabinski (http://www.emilydrabinski.com/), and Jennifer Vinopal (http://vinopal.org/), to name a few.

of reprisal or rejection. To create that safe culture, we need to address diversity in concrete terms, supported by inclusive policies, procedures, and practices. In the larger context, we need to be more honest about the real challenges facing libraries, and our relevance in the communities we serve. We need to change the way we make collective decisions such that community-supported solutions are the default, benefiting everyone not just now but also for the long term. To a greater degree, feminist-led libraries can do the work that reflects the values we hold.

The feminist framework, then, is integral to my leadership practice and is the filter through which I critically self-reflect and determine the "right thing to do", both on a day-to-day basis and when considering the larger issues that face librarianship. While my framework continues to grow and evolve the more I read and learn from others, at its core is the truthfulness of my lived experience which remains my most trusted point of reference. Accepting the lived experience as valid and relevant to my practice is essential and provides the stable foundation for building a framework that can stand on its own. In this chapter, I've attempted to reflect on my path to feminism and library leadership and have found parallels in my personal experience and in the issues I see confronting librarianship. Silence characterized my way of survival, and internalizing patriarchal marginalization was my mode of being. The same silence and internalizing of oppressive systems is evident in the library profession. In both, there is a conflict and dissonance between behavior and our sense of identity, and in both the disconnect has, I would argue, led to crisis. For me, the crisis came at the moment of becoming the director of the library, and having to decide whether I was going to lead from a place of oppression or from a place of transparency and authenticity. For the library community, the crisis hinges on the question of whether we can answer, with honesty, who it is we are working for—the interests of the establishment (institutions or individuals) or the betterment of the greater good now and in the future. I hope this exploration contributes to an evolving environment in which we have more discussions about our varied experiences, and to valuing the different perspectives our individual experiences bring to librarianship. I'd like to hear us talk about how different ways of practicing librarianship can sustain all of us, and have this reflected back to the communities we serve. I'm inspired by the words of Toni Morrison:

> I tell my students, 'When you get these jobs that you have been so brilliantly trained for, just remember that your real job is that if you are free, you need to free somebody else. If you have some power, then your job is to empower somebody else. This is not just a grab-bag candy game.[10]

The real job of a feminist leader is simple: free yourself in order to free and empower others; free our libraries in order to empower those we serve. I know I am not alone in wanting this to be the kind of librarianship I wish to practice and be part of.

---

10 Toni Morrison, interview by Pam Houston, "The Truest Eye," *O, The Oprah Magazine*, November 2003, 212.

BIBLIOGRAPHY

Freire, Paulo. *Pedagogy of the Oppressed*, 30th anniversary ed. New York: Continuum International, 2001.

hooks, bell. *Feminism is for Everybody: Passionate Politics.* Cambridge: South End Press, 2000.

Morrison, Toni. "The Truest Eye," Interview by Pam Houston. *O, The Oprah Magazine*, November 2003.

Nagy Hesse-Biber, Sharlene, "Feminist Research: Exploring, Interrogating, and Transforming the Interconnections of Epistemology, Methodology, and Method" in *Handbook of Feminist Research: Theory and Praxis,* edited by Sharlene Nagy Hesse-Biber, 2. Los Angeles: Sage Publications, 2012.

Wunker, Erin. *Notes from a Feminist Killjoy: Essays on Everyday Life.* Toronto: BookThug, 2016.

A Feminist Critique of Servant Leadership

Lisa Richmond

Augustine of Hippo's famous remark about the elusive nature of time—"What, then, is time? I know well enough what it is, provided that nobody asks me; but if I am asked what it is and try to explain, I am baffled,"—may be applied with equal justice to the elusive nature of leadership.[1] As one leadership theorist has remarked, "Of all the hazy and confounding areas in social psychology, leadership theory undoubtedly contends for top nomination."[2] The great German sociologist and philosopher Max Weber made important contributions to leadership theory a century ago,[3] but a study of leadership grounded in contemporary social-scientific methodology is only a few decades old and as such is in an early stage of development. Some researchers conceptualize leadership fundamentally as a *process*—an extended interaction between the leader and followers to achieve particular

---

1 Augustine of Hippo, *Confessions*, 11.14, trans. R.S. Pine-Coffin (New York: Penguin, 1961), 264.

2 W. G. Bennis, "Leadership Theory and Administrative Behavior: The Problem of Authority," *Administrative Science Quarterly* 4 (1959): 259–301, Doi:10.2307/2390911, quoted in A. H. Eagly and J. Antonakis, "Leadership," Chapter 18, 571–592 in *APA Handbook of Personality and Social Psychology, Vol. 1. Attitudes and Social Cognition*, ed. M. Mikulincer and P. R. Shaver (Washington, DC: American Psychological Association, 2015). Quotation on 571.

3 See for example M. Weber, "Politics as a Vocation" and "The Sociology of Charismatic Authority" in *From Max Weber: Essays in Sociology*, trans. and ed. H. H. Gerth and C. Wright Mills (New York: Oxford University Press, 1946).

ends. Other researchers view it primarily as a set of *traits* that reside in leaders, perhaps innately. Others study leadership as a set of *skills* that enable the leader to accomplish certain outcomes. According to this theory, one does not need to be a "born leader," since it is possible to develop the skills or capabilities for effective leadership.

A fourth avenue of research has been the theoretical development and empirical testing of various leadership *styles*, understood as "relatively stable patterns of behavior" that leaders exhibit.[4] As such, this approach focuses not on a leader's innate qualities or on capabilities, but on how a leader acts. Robert Greenleaf, a former executive at AT&T in the United States, is credited with positing servant leadership as one such leadership style. Servant leadership has gained widespread support in contemporary North American society for its refreshing perspective that leadership should be concerned fundamentally with service rather than power. Organizations that recruit and cultivate "servant leaders," it is argued, may be more likely to avoid the disasters that occur at the hands of self-aggrandizing leaders. Servant leadership has been recommended as a style particularly suited to the profession of librarianship. To take one example, librarian Michael Germano has written:

> The concept of servant leadership underscores the critical role of service to both the organization and its customers. . . . Because libraries primarily exist as service organizations, servant leadership should be revisited and more closely examined by librarians, since it may represent both a strong cultural and tactical fit for libraries. . . . ideally suited to libraries.[5]

Servant leadership theory is important to critique within the academic library context for several reasons. One reason is that our profession and our institutional mission are often expressed in terms of service to our universities or to library users as individuals, as the quotation above makes clear. The term *user*, which has for good reason

---

4 A. H. Eagly and M. C. Johannesen-Schmidt, "The Leadership Styles of Women and Men," *Journal of Social Issues* 57.4 (2001): 781–797. Quotation on 781.

5 M. Germano, "Leadership and Value Co-Creation in Academic Libraries," In *Leadership in Academic Libraries Today: Connecting Theory to Practice*, ed. B. L. Eden and J. C Fagan (Lanham, MD: Rowman & Littlefield, 2014), 118. See also P. Katopol, "Everybody Wins: Servant-Leadership." *Library Leadership & Management* 29.4 (2015): 1–7; F. M. Anzalone, "Servant Leadership: A New Model for Law Library Leaders," *Law Library Journal* 99.4 (2007): 793–812; and R. Moniz, J. Henry, and J. Eshleman, *Fundamentals of the Academic Library Liaison* (Chicago: Neil-Schuman/ALA, 2014), 72.

replaced *patron*, establishes a semantic penumbra of *service* over the academic library setting, even if this word does not explicitly appear in departmental names, job titles, or descriptions of work. Although one can argue that education as a whole is fundamentally about service, professors conceptualize their work primarily in terms of teaching and research and only secondarily in terms of service (to the institution, the community, or the profession). To the extent that librarians, whether they have faculty status at their institution or not, view themselves or are viewed by others primarily as service providers, the implication is that the work done by librarians is ancillary to, in the service of, the real work of the university rather than one expression of that real work. This is a problem if librarians desire to attain full equality and status as faculty members at their institutions. The adoption of servant leadership discourse in the academic library setting may make this goal more difficult to attain. Indeed, such a goal seems not to be in the minds of the LIS authors just cited, who explicitly recommend servant leadership style for its perceived congruity with academic librarianship understood as a service profession.[6]

Servant leadership theory requires critique in our profession for another reason as well: its implications for gender equality. Harris's classic work *Librarianship: The Erosion of a Woman's Profession* argues that since librarianship is strongly perceived as a female profession, the status of librarianship and the status of women are closely linked. Various approaches may be tried for elevating the status of the profession, but none will ultimately be successful, in her view, until the status of women itself improves. Whether one agrees with Harris on this point or not, her argument is that our focus should be directed first to the status of women rather than to that of the profession; when we improve the status of women, we will find that the status of our profession improves also.[7] I argue in this chapter that servant leadership theory does not advance the status of women and is in fact inimical to this goal.

---

6 Kara Malenfant is one exception. She writes, "I do not believe thinking in these terms is in the best interests of academic librarians. I believe servant and follower frames are not useful for librarians given the hierarchical mindset of the academy. . . . Those who think of themselves as servant, assistant, or follower have erected powerful mental models that can indicate a lack of mutuality [with professors] and the belief that they are powerless." K. J. Malenfant, "Understanding Faculty Perceptions of the Future: Action Research for Academic Librarians" (PhD diss., Antioch University, 2011) 39–40. Retrieved from http://aura.antioch.edu/etds/19/.

7 R. M. Harris, *Librarianship: The Erosion of a Woman's Profession* (Norwood, NJ: Ablex, 1992).

Overview of Servant Leadership Theory and Research

In *The Servant as Leader*, Greenleaf describes how his theory originated in reading Herman Hesse's novel *The Journey to the East*,[8] a work of psychic mysticism in which a group's servant, named Leo, is revealed through the course of the narrative to be the group's actual leader, without whom the group cannot function.[9] Building on this initial idea, Greenleaf posited that the only legitimate authority in human affairs is that which followers freely accord to leaders based on these leaders' servant-like qualities. The servant role comes first, and the leadership role is derived from it. The desire to serve precedes the desire to lead and remains the foundational motive throughout the entire experience. As such, servant leadership is a paradoxical leadership theory, in that it is fundamentally a theory of service and not of leadership *per se*. It is unique among theories of leadership style in its grounding in the leader's motivation. "The motivational element of servant leadership (i.e., to serve first) portrays a fundamental presupposition which distinguishes [it] from other leadership [styles]."[10]

According to Greenleaf, servant leaders seek to ensure that the "highest-priority needs" of their followers are met. These needs are health, wisdom, freedom, and autonomy, among others. Leaders have their personal right and claim to leadership only by taking as their guiding concern their followers' growth in these areas and in their own servant leadership qualities. Greenleaf argues that true leaders must be first a servant of those whom they lead: "The only authority deserving one's allegiance is that which is freely and knowingly granted by the led to the leader in response to, and in proportion to, the clearly evident servant stature of the leader."[11]

---

8 H. Hesse, *The Journey to the East*, trans. H. Rosner (New York: Farrar, Straus and Giroux, 1968).

9 R. K. Greenleaf, *The Servant as Leader* (Cambridge, MA: Center for Applied Studies, 1970).

10 S. Sendjaya and J. C. Sarros, "Servant Leadership: Its Origin, Development, and Application in Organizations," *Journal of Leadership & Organizational Studies* 9.2 (2002): 57–64. Quotation on 60.

11 Greenleaf, *The Servant as Leader*, 4.

Greenleaf's primary successor, Larry Spears, has used Greenleaf's writings to identify ten servant leader attributes:[12]

Listening. While listening, as part of communication, has always been considered important for leadership, servant leaders are especially concerned to listen carefully and receptively to others at all levels in the organization.

Empathy. The servant leader seeks to understand and appreciate each person's uniqueness, motivation, and situation.

Healing. Servant leaders seek to heal and find wholeness for themselves and others.

Awareness. Emphasis is placed on fostering self-awareness, other-awareness, and greater clarification of beliefs and values, in order to reach the most holistic understanding possible.

Persuasion. Rather than relying on coercive or positional power, the servant leader seeks to persuade and build consensus.

Conceptualization. Servant leaders seek to foster broad, long-term understandings of situations and contexts, and encourage their followers to make dreams and plans.

Foresight. This is the ability to reflect on and learn from the past, and anticipate likely outcomes of the present and future.

Stewardship. Servant leadership views all authority as stewardship, in which trust is placed in the leader to provide for and protect what has been entrusted, for the general good.

Commitment to the growth of people. People are ends, not means. Practically, servant leadership tends to emphasize opportunities for professional development, shared decision-making, work-life balance, and other practices that are viewed as empowering to followers.

Building community. The servant leader seeks to focus deep and local relationships.

---

12 See L. C. Spears, ed. *Reflections on Leadership: How Robert K. Greenleaf's Theory of Servant-leadership Influenced Today's Top Management Thinkers* (New York: Wiley, 1995), and L. C. Spears and M. Lawrence, eds. *Focus on Leadership: Servant-leadership for the Twenty-first Century* (New York: Wiley, 2002).

Barbuto and Wheeler built on Spears and his work with Lawrence by adding the attribute of *calling*. Distilling the eleven attributes to their fundamental expressions, they established a five-dimensional construct of servant leadership:[13]

Altruistic calling: the desire to make a positive difference in the lives of others and put their needs ahead of one's own.

Emotional healing: the ability to help others to overcome hardship.

Wisdom: the ability to be aware of one's context and foresee implications for the future.

Persuasive mapping: the ability to reason well about the present and future, develop a vision, and persuade others to follow it.

Organizational stewardship: the ability to lead the organization in contributing to the well-being of the community or society of which it forms a part.

In their summary of the historical expressions of servant leadership, business professors Sendjaya and Sarros note that various leaders from ancient times to the present have acknowledged servanthood as the basis of leadership, but they suggest that Jesus Christ is the figure who both taught and modeled servant leadership as an ideal type to the greatest degree. Relying on evidence in the Christian scriptures, these researchers point to instances in which Jesus taught his followers that "whoever wants to become great among you must be your servant" and symbolically demonstrated his own servanthood by choosing to wash his disciples' feet in an expression of humility.[14] My own encounter with the concept of servant leadership occurred first within religious organizational settings, and for some time I assumed that it was based primarily on Jesus' teaching and appealed primarily to (some) Christians. Of course, many originally Christian themes, including the idea of Jesus' servanthood, have been "secularized" into Western culture, so that those without Christian beliefs may also find servant leadership to align with their values. But it was only when I began to read broadly in the field of leadership research and theory

---

13 J. E. Barbuto and D. W. Wheeler, "Scale Development and Construct Clarification of Servant Leadership," *Group & Organization Management* 31.3 (2006): 300–26.

14 See Bible, New International Version. Gospel of Mark 10 and Gospel of John 13.

that I observed the wide and diverse adoption of servant leadership and noted that Greenleaf drew much more on existentialist themes from Albert Camus, and on Hesse's character Leo in *The Journey to the East,* than on any specifically Christian material. Regardless of what its originating sources actually are, this form of leadership now has widespread support among those who seek greater personal meaning beyond mere careerism, and among leaders who seek greater personal meaning beyond mere exercise of power.

Greenleaf points to the great potential influence of servant leaders by considering the example of John Woolman, the eighteenth-century American Quaker who led his church to be the first to formally denounce and forbid slavery among its members. Woolman achieved this not by protest or attempts to impose his own sense of justice, but by leading the Quakers' own moral sense through persuasion and value clarification. Greenleaf suggests that if there had been only fifty or even five such anti-slavery leaders in the United States during this time, disaster would have been averted: "Perhaps we would not have had the war with its 600,000 casualties and the impoverishment of the South, and with the resultant vexing social problem that is at fever heat 100 years later with no end in sight." The "advantages" of change "by convincement rather than coercion . . . are obvious."[15]

Behavioral scientists Joseph and Winston surveyed university students who had employment experience and found a strong positive correlation between the students' perceptions of servant leadership in their organizations and their degree of trust in the organization's leader(s).[16] Mayer, Bardes, and Piccolo surveyed employed undergraduate students to determine the degree to which servant leadership actually satisfies follower needs. These researchers found a positive correlation between perceptions of servant leadership in the organization and followers' overall job satisfaction and need satisfaction in such areas as wisdom and autonomy.[17] Surveying

---

15 Greenleaf, *The Servant as Leader*, 21–22.

16 E. E. Joseph and B. E. Winston, "A Correlation of Servant Leadership, Leader Trust, and Organizational Trust," *Leadership & Organizational Development Journal* 26.1/2 (2005): 6–22.

17 D. M. Mayer, M. Bardes, and R. F. Piccolo, "Do Servant-leaders Help Satisfy Follower Needs? An Organizational Justice Perspective," *European Journal of Work and Organizational Psychology* 17.2 (2008): 180–197.

employees in various workplace settings, Laub also found that job satisfaction correlates positively with perception of servant leadership in the organization.[18]

Servant leadership may be appealing, but is it effective? Organizational success, however this is defined, is generally considered to be the purpose of leadership in an organizational context. Servant leadership theory has not in fact established how meeting the needs of one's followers produces organizational success, and in some cases its theorists even seems unconcerned to do so. While it is clear that servant leadership focuses on meeting followers' needs for autonomy, growth, and other psychic goods, the way in which the organization benefits when leaders seek to meet these needs is unclear. Some theorists suggest that servant leadership produces organizational wisdom, and thus optimal choices that in turn produce organizational success.[19] Others suggest that servant leadership produces trust, which in turn enhances the organization's ability to reach its goals,[20] or that it brings order and meaning to followers' lives, producing energy and accomplishment.[21] Still others suggest that servant leadership, while meeting the needs of followers, may subordinate organizational success to those needs in such a way that organizational success does not occur.[22]

Women and Leadership

The research briefly described in the section above suggests that servant leadership benefits or is appreciated by one's followers on a personal level, regardless of whether it actually promotes the attainment of

---

18 J. A. Laub, "Assessing the Servant Organization: Development of the Servant Organizational Leadership Assessment (SOLA) Instrument" (PhD diss., Florida Atlantic University, 1999). Retrieved from Dissertations and Theses Fulltext. (AAT 9921922).

19 Barbuto and Wheeler, "Scale Development."

20 J. Lowe, "Trust: The Invaluable Asset." In *Insights on Leadership*, ed. L. C. Spears, 68–76 (New York: Wiley, 1998).

21 D. Chappel, "*Fortune*'s 'Best Companies to Work For' Embrace Servant Leadership," *The Servant Leader* 5 (2000), n. p.

22 B. N. Smith, R. V. Montagno, and T. N. Kuzmenko, "Transformational and Servant Leadership: Context and Contextual Comparisons," *Journal of Leadership & Organizational Studies* 10.4 (2004): 80–91.

organizational goals. Yet more recent research complicates these positive perceptions by shedding light on the importance of context for the success of servant leadership style. The context in which a servant leader functions includes such aspects as the organizational and societal culture, the degree of follower receptivity, and many other factors. Researchers Liden, Wayne, Zhao, and Henderson,[23] and Meuser, Liden, Wayne, and Henderson[24] have found that some employees do not value or appreciate a servant leadership style enacted by those above them in the organization. Context, of course, also includes gender—the gender of the leader and that of the follower(s).

On first consideration, servant leadership may seem appealing as a leadership style for women or for feminists regardless of gender. It may even appear as a style that aligns particularly well with the "ethic of care" that is frequently invoked in feminist contexts.[25] Yet this model of leadership raises questions for the status of women that have not been adequately explored. There has as yet been little research into questions such as whether servant leadership appeals more to women than to men (whether as leaders or as followers), whether it is viewed as more appropriate for women than for men, or whether women leaders feel more organizational pressure to use it than do men. And crucially, what are the actual results, for gender equality as opposed to organizational success, when servant leadership theory is applied in organizational settings? In the absence of empirical evidence, we can begin by developing some theoretical constructs. We can examine what is known about gender and about leadership and then seek to apply that evidence in a theoretical way to gender and servant leadership in particular.

In the field of leadership and gender in the North American context, one of the most well-established empirical findings is that

---

23 R. C. Liden, S. J. Wayne, H. Zhao, and D. Henderson, "Servant Leadership: Development of a Multidimensional Measure and Multi-Level Assessment," *Leadership Quarterly* 19.2 (2008): 161–177.

24 J. D. Meuser, R. C. Liden, S. J. Wayne, and D. J. Henderson, "Is Servant Leadership Always a Good Thing? The Moderating Influence of Servant Leadership Prototype" (paper presented at the meeting of the Academy of Management, San Antonio, Texas, August, 2011), cited in P. G. Northouse, *Leadership: Theory and Practice*, 6th ed. (Los Angeles: Sage, 2013), 227.

25 See C. Gilligan, *In a Different Voice* (Cambridge, MA: Harvard University Press, 1982).

competence and likeability are positively correlated for male leaders and negatively correlated for female leaders. In other words, the more a male leader is perceived as competent, the more he is perceived as likeable (and vice versa). The more a female leader is perceived as competent, the less she is perceived as likeable (and vice versa). This is not true in each individual case, but it is true in the aggregate.[26] This finding, often referred to as the female leader's double bind, is so well established in the research literature that it is no longer in dispute.[27] Some researchers have now shifted their focus to seeking to uncover *why* it is so.

The theory explaining the female leader's double bind that has received the most support in recent years, Role Congruity Theory, offers the following sequence of ideas. Over the course of their socialization, human beings develop implicit cognitive associations with regard to all sorts of variables. Gender and leadership are two such variables, among many others. Such cognitive associations are constructed over time and experience, based on the frequently occurring, "typical," and therefore "normal" conditions present across a person's experiences in dominant social settings. These associations are also constructed through the reception of explicit and implicit teaching and modeling by others. By adulthood, a highly developed web of associations, held strongly, weakly, or somewhere in between, exists in each person's mind. The Implicit Association Test, developed by researchers at Harvard University, is one well-known instrument that can be self-administered and enable individual persons to assess the strength of their own implicit associations between gender, race, and various other human characteristics.[28]

Implicit associations are essentially cognitive shortcuts. The mind's ability to form implicit associations contributes positively to personal and societal well-being to the extent that it enables the mind to respond automatically or habitually to expected conditions, thereby

---

26 Similarly, my references throughout this chapter to *female* and to *male* are meant as general categories. I do not argue that these categories apply equally well to every individual person.

27 This research finding is prominently discussed in, among other works, I. Bohnet, *What Works: Gender Equality by Design* (Cambridge, MA: Harvard University Press, 2016) and A. H. Eagly and L. L. Carli, *Through the Labyrinth: The Truth about How Women Become Leaders* (Boston: Harvard Business School Press, 2007).

28 Project Implicit, Implicit Association Test. Retrieved from implicit.harvard.edu.

freeing the mind to focus on the unexpected conditions that typically require more effort. Cognitive shortcuts are harmful, however, to the extent that they serve to reinforce existing conditions by arming the mind in favor of such conditions, regardless of how these conditions came into existence and how just (fair, equitable) and desirable they actually are.[29]

When a person's implicit associations map easily onto the actual conditions of a given situation, the experience is a comfortable one. For example, when a person encounters a basketball player who is tall, no cognitive dissonance is experienced between the mental category *basketball player* and the category *tall*, since these are already closely associated in people's minds.[30] When one's implicit associations map poorly onto given conditions, however, cognitive stress and resistance can arise—all the more so when one or more of the categories in play are already vested with importance in the person's mind. It must be remembered that these associations, and the comfort or stress that are evoked, are largely implicit. That is, they occur on the subconscious level and are rarely consciously chosen, felt, or reflected on.

Most people implicitly perceive gender to be the most important, or salient, way of categorizing human beings:

> People instantly categorize individuals as male or female. In the rare cases in which this instant recognition fails, people keep probing until they resolve the ambiguity of an androgynous appearance. In fact, sex provides the strongest basis of classifying people: it trumps race, age, and occupation in the speed and ubiquity of categorizing others. Classifying a person as male or female evokes mental associations, or expectations, about masculine and feminine qualities. These associations are pervasive and influential even when people are not aware of them.[31]

---

29 Possible answers to such questions lie outside the scope of this chapter. Eagly and Carli's *Through the Labyrinth* is a good resource for further exploration, particularly for what may be termed the argument from evolutionary psychology.

30 Height, of course, is another characteristic of human beings that is invested with implicit associations. While this chapter focuses on challenges specific to women in leadership, it must be remembered that men may experience challenges also, when one or more of their personal characteristics map poorly onto leadership expectations. I am reminded of a comment once made by a male university president, who remarked that the first time he attended a national event for university presidents, "I felt like I had walked into a room of basketball players." Most of these presidents were taller-than-average men.

31 Eagly and Carli, *Through the Labyrinth*, 85, and citing additional research.

North Americans generally associate the category *female* with communal qualities such as kindness, sensitivity, and other-directedness, and the category *male* with agentic qualities such as assertion, self-confidence, and ambition. That is, people in our society consider that women, in general, *are* or *should be* communal, and that men, in general, *are* or *should be* agentic. At the same time, they associate the category *leader* with agentic qualities.[32] Thus the categories of *female* and *leader* mesh poorly with one another, while the categories of *male* and *leader* mesh well. In the unconscious minds of followers, therefore, for a female leader either the *female* or the *leader* needs to give way to the other. The result is as described above: the female leader is perceived either as a "successful female" (communal) or as a "successful leader" (agentic) but not as both together. Former Canadian prime minister Kim Campbell described her experience of the female leader's double bind as follows:

> I don't have a traditionally female way of speaking. I don't end my sentences with a question mark. I'm quite assertive. If I didn't speak the way I do, I wouldn't have been seen as a leader. But my way of speaking may have grated on people who were not used to hearing it from a woman. It was the right way for a leader to speak, but it wasn't the right way for a woman to speak. It goes against type.[33]

The female leader faces a quandary: will she be a "successful female" or a "successful leader"? In most cases, what she wants is to be both.

FEMINIST CRITIQUE OF SERVANT LEADERSHIP

We are now in a position to apply these principles and conclusions about gender and leadership to servant leadership theory specifically. Servant leadership essentially seeks to reframe leadership by bringing it into relation with some *servant*-like qualities (e.g., *altruism*), thereby creating the oft-cited paradox of servant leadership—in other words, the ill-fitting but intentional confluence of the implicit mental categories of *servant* and of *leader*. We cannot avoid the observation that some of the *servant*-associated qualities that are specified for this

---

32 A. H. Eagly and S. J. Karau, "Role Congruity Theory of Prejudice toward Female Leaders," *Psychological Review* 109.3 (2002): 573–598.

33 K. Campbell as quoted in Eagly and Carli, *Through the Labyrinth*, 102.

leadership style appear similar to or the same as implicitly *female*-associated qualities (*listening, empathy, community*, and so forth). Does this mean, therefore, that the double bind of the female leader may be overcome by the widespread application of this leadership style, that servant leadership is good news for gender equality? There are several possible outcomes. One is that the category *leader* can indeed be explicitly reframed or expanded in such a way that, over time, the implicit dissonance between *leader* and *female* decreases. Another outcome, however, is that the categories *servant* and *female* may become more closely associated than ever.

If we look again at Spears's characteristics of a servant leader, listed earlier in this chapter, we observe that not all of these characteristics in fact map easily on to the implicit category *female*. Those that map well are *listening, empathy, healing, awareness*, and *commitment to others' growth*, but the remaining qualities in the list are ones that arguably map equally well to *female* and to *male*. The characteristic of *conceptualization* arguably maps best to *male*. Similarly, Barbuto and Wheeler's five-point distillation of Spears's list include *altruistic calling* and *emotional healing*, two qualities that map well to *female*, but for the remaining qualities the gender mapping is either neutral or perhaps favors *male*. Thus it would be mistaken to consider servant leadership as a *female*-identified leadership style, with a predominantly communal rather than agentic orientation. While servant leadership does indeed differ from a traditionally *male*-identified style of leadership (one that is popularly referred to as "command-and-control" or "top-down"), servant leadership style draws on both *female* and *male*, both communal and agentic, categories, and not on *female* alone or predominantly.

We have already examined the result that occurs when female leaders exhibit what are implicitly perceived as male qualities: they may be viewed as more competent leaders, but they may be less well liked. Likability is correlated with how well a man or a woman fulfills the expected gender norm that exists in the minds of others, that is, how "successfully male" or "successfully female" the person appears and behaves from the point of view of one's followers. Dislike generates resistance in followers, which in turn affects the female leader's ability to succeed. When male leaders exhibit qualities that are more typically viewed as female, perceptions of likability seem not to be affected.[34] Additionally, Johnson, Murphy, Zewski, and Reichard examined followers' perceptions of male and female leaders in terms of these leaders' strength, sensitivity, effectiveness, and likeability, finding that neither male nor female followers "rated sensitivity as being important to their leader's effectiveness when that leader was a man"[35] and further that

> The sensitive female leader was liked less than the strong male leader, [since,] by being a woman, the female leader has already violated one leadership prototype, because she is presumably low in masculinity. So, regardless of her behavior she is already at a disadvantage compared to her male counterpart. . . . For effectiveness, we found that all leaders [assessed in this study] were seen as equally effective, except the strong female leader who was [seen as] the least effective. Although role congruity theory would predict that sensitive male leaders would be perceived as ineffective, they may have demonstrated their prototypicality by simply being male. Further, participants may believe that he is still strong enough to be a leader, just because he is a man.[36]

What may occur when male and female leaders employ a servant leadership style, or when servant leadership is urged upon male and female leaders as the desired style to employ, the effect on male leaders may be neutral (or possibly beneficial—to the extent that they become less associated with the negatively perceived aspects of the command-and-control style), while the effect on female leaders may be to associate them more closely with the *female* and less closely with the *male* or gender-neutral characteristics of this style. As such, servant leadership style may reinforce the existing barriers to female leadership success.

Viewed in this light, much of what has been written in favor of servant leadership begins to take on more troubling implications for gender equality. For example, some theorists have understood Greenleaf to hold that "the servant assumes a non-focal position within

---

34 See also Eagly and Carli, *Through the Labyrinth*, 104, citing additional research.

35 S. K. Johnson, S. E. Murphy, S. Zewski, and R. J. Reichard, "The Strong Sensitive Type: Effects of Gender Stereotypes and Leader Prototypes on the Evaluation of Male and Female Leaders," *Organizational Behavior and Human Decision Processes* 106.1 (2008): 39–60. Quotation on 50.

36 Ibid., 45.

a group, providing resources and support without an expectation of acknowledgement."[37] If this is true, women's use of servant leadership can lead to their continued subordination according to traditional gender roles, since these activities map well to *female*. Smith, Montagno, and Kuzmenko state that "Through repeated servant behaviors, these individuals eventually emerge as pivotal for group survival and are thrust into a leadership position."[38] The assumption that this result will occur routinely for women is doubtful, however, given what is known about the challenges that women face in attaining leadership recognition.[39]

This theme is taken up by Eicher-Catt, who finds in servant leadership theory an entrenchment of sex-based power relations. In her view, "the apposition of 'servant' with 'leader' . . . [does] not neutralize gender bias but accentuate[s] it."[40] She suggests that since *leader* is a *male*-identified concept, its close coupling with *servant* causes this second concept to become *female*-identified. Further, the seemingly benign association with *servant* "inhibits whatever negative connotation 'leader' invokes," potentially rendering the (male) leader that much more powerful.[41] In her view, servant leadership theory fundamentally instantiates a relational logic of opposition and hierarchy with strongly gendered overtones.

> Servant leadership represents a rhetorical discourse that reifies a historically sanctioned, prescribed ethic—in this case an androcentric one—that is increasingly masked by its spiritual connotations. . . . While on the surface the language or logos of S-L appears to promote an innocent ethic of resistance to standardized, perhaps oppressive, leadership practices, it operates by a logic of rhetorical substitution that maintains, or at least can maintain, those oppressive practices.[42]

---

37 Smith, Montagno, and Kuzmenko, "Transformational and Servant Leadership," 81.

38 Ibid., 81.

39 Eagly and Carli, *Through the Labyrinth*.

40 D. Eicher-Catt, "The Myth of Servant-leadership: A Feminist Perspective," *Women and Language* 28.1 (2005): 17–25. Quotation on 17.

41 Ibid., 19.

42 Ibid., 23.

As a result, Eicher-Catt concludes, servant leadership's "rhetorical move negates any opportunity to create more two-way communicative relationships that might advance more egalitarian and authentic encounters."[43] If servant leadership style serves to reinforce gender-norm stereotypes and thus gender inequality, its aim to "nurture individual growth . . . recognizing followers' contributions and helping them realize their human potential"[44] becomes a more elusive goal.

As noted at the outset of this chapter, servant leadership is a style, that is, a pattern of behavior. Unlike traits or skills, which are actual characteristics of a person, it is possible for behavior to be enacted artificially. One's behavior can be a performance rather than the expression of one's real self. While servant leadership theory emphatically posits that it is not a technique that can be adopted or discarded as strategy seems to dictate, there is in fact no means by which followers or other observers could confirm or disconfirm this supposition. The theory takes as a given that servant leaders act the way they do because they believe it is the right way. Such a belief therefore invests this leadership style with unique strength and moral standing, and from this basis, I suggest, flows all the power of this leadership style. Servant leaders, taken as such on faith, seem to be rooted in a personal commitment that deeply aligns with their own values and beliefs, and their apparent sincerity and integrity may have a powerful effect on followers.

It is with this crucial assumption of the servant leader's authenticity that researchers such as J. W. Graham argue for servant leadership style as surpassing charismatic/transformational leadership (another leadership style, with which servant leadership is frequently compared) in moral status by its emphasis on serving individual rather than organizational needs and on serving the needs of those who are marginalized. She points out that charisma can be used for malevolent as well as benevolent purposes, and she criticizes theorists for having mostly "neglect[ed] the moral hazards involved" in the charismatic leadership style.[45] Graham also notes a fundamental problem within charismatic/transformational leadership theory: it tells followers that

---

43 Ibid., 20.

44 Northouse, *Leadership,* 230.

45 J. W. Graham, "Servant-leadership in Organizations: Inspirational and Moral," *Leadership Quarterly* 2.2 (1991): 105–119. Quotation on 106.

personal growth and transformation are necessary, but it cannot tell them *why* in terms that are personally meaningful—the well-being and success of the organization, not the followers, is what ultimately matters. Servant leadership, by contrast, invokes personal growth for the sake of the followers' benefit. Graham does not express a concern that the congruity between a leader's inward convictions and outward behavior is unverifiable outside the leader's own conscience.

Servant leadership style can therefore be an expression of a leader's true self and noblest motivations—or it can be a highly effective technique, involving at least some degree of dissimulation.[46] If servant leadership theory presupposes ambition, it may be fundamentally understood as a technique for creating more-willing followers so that, by disciplining one's desires, one can, in the end, attain those desires more fully. It is interesting to return to the biblical passage, cited earlier, with this possibility in mind. Jesus told his disciples that *"whoever wants to become great among you* must be your servant" (emphasis added), and he did so because two of his disciples had asked him for positions of high status and power:

> Then James and John, the sons of Zebedee, came to him. "Teacher," they said, "we want you to do for us whatever we ask." "What do you want me to do for you?" he asked. They replied, "Let one of us sit at your right and the other at your left in your glory." . . . When the ten [other disciples] heard about this, they became indignant with James and John. Jesus called them together and said, "You know that those who are regarded as rulers of the Gentiles lord it over them, and their high officials exercise authority over them. Not so with you. Instead,

---

46 Although I am stressing the potential duplicity that I find inherent in this leadership style, I want to emphasize that pretending, or "behaving as though," is not necessarily wrong or worthy of contempt. In fact, it can play a central role in the development of actual goodness. In his *Nicomachean Ethics*, Aristotle argues that one's character is formed by repeatedly acting in a certain way; such action eventually becomes a part of the person's true self. An "active condition" (in Greek, *hexis*) "is any way in which one deliberately holds oneself in relation to feelings and desires, once it becomes a constant part of oneself. For example, fear is a feeling, and lack of confidence is a predisposition to feel fear; both are passive conditions. Cowardice or courage are active conditions one may develop toward them. One's character is made up of active conditions. Hence this is one of the most important words in the *Nicomachean Ethics*, and the foundation of Aristotle's understanding of human responsibility." Joe Sachs, introduction to Aristotle, *Nicomachean Ethics*, trans. Joe Sachs (Newburyport, MA: Focus, 2002), 201.

whoever wants to become great among you must be your servant, and whoever wants to be first must be slave of all."[47]

In this passage, as in many others throughout the Gospels, the meaning of Jesus' teaching is hard to interpret. But one plausible meaning, or part of the meaning, that Jesus intended for his disciples is that a servant leadership style may help to rectify arrogance and other personal characteristics that produce low quality of leadership and that may be harmful to the self and to others.

While such qualities can be present in women as well as men, servant leadership theory has developed within a historical reality in which male arrogance, self-aggrandizement, or abuse of power is the implicitly identified problem, if only because, historically, leaders have overwhelmingly been male. As already noted, when a male leader enacts a servant leadership style, the effect on followers can be positive and the leader may suffer no diminution of his authority or appeal. As such, the male leader can be more successful than he otherwise would be—and this is all to the good, if the ends that the male leader is pursuing are just and right (as the case of John Woolman, cited earlier, exemplifies). But if a female leader applies this style, the result can be problematic. Servant leadership as a theory fundamentally assumes a context in which the leader is already perceived as powerful or potentially so, and then reins in or relinquishes that power to some extent. The theory therefore takes its beginning at a place that cannot be assumed, or that is not typically the case, for the female leader, whether in the library profession or some other. If a female leader is not already perceived as possessing power, then her servant leadership may be perceived as weakness, and this of course undermines the very goal of becoming an effective leader.

Instead of recommending servant leadership in the academic librarian context, as the LIS authors cited earlier have done, a better approach may be to identify and cultivate traits or skills in both sexes that have been shown through other research as being effective for good leadership. As Eagly and Carli note, when we shift our focus from pursuing a leadership style to examining instead "the personality traits that are in fact correlated with [effective] leadership, and we evaluate whether they are more prevalent in one sex than the other," the current state of research in this area suggests that "the psychological

---

47 Bible, New International Version. Gospel of Mark 10:35–45.

portrait of good leaders is neither masculine nor feminine but includes traits from both of these domains in approximately equal measure."[48] Such qualities include self-confidence, persistence, sociability, responsibility, and initiative, among others.[49] Futhermore, Barbuto and Gifford conclude from their research that "no differences were found between men and women in the utilization of communal and agentic servant leadership behaviors," and that "male and females are equally capable of utilizing both agentic and communal leadership behaviors."[50] If these findings are true, academic librarianship should drop the servant leadership "paradox," with its potential to further instantiate gender inequality, and focus instead on encouraging the combination of qualities that men and women are equally capable of and that contribute positively to leadership success.[51]

---

48 Eagly and Carli, *Through the Labyrinth*, 29.

49 Northouse, *Leadership*, 22.

50 J. E. Barbuto and G. T. Gifford, "Examining Gender Differences of Servant Leadership: An Analysis of the Agentic and Communal Properties of the Servant Leadership Questionnaire," *Journal of Leadership Education* 9.2 (2010): 4–21. Quotations on 14–15.

51 I wish to express my gratitude to Nancy Falciani-White, Andy Tooley, and especially Nick Maroules for their helpful comments on an earlier version of this chapter.

BIBLIOGRAPHY

Anzalone, F. M., "Servant Leadership: A New Model for Law Library Leaders." *Law Library Journal* 99.4 (2007): 793–812.

Aristotle, *Nicomachean Ethics*, translated by Joe Sachs. Newburyport, MA: Focus, 2002.

Augustine of Hippo, *Confessions*, translated by R. S. Pine-Coffin. New York: Penguin, 1961.

Barbuto, J. E. and G. T. Gifford, "Examining Gender Differences of Servant Leadership: An Analysis of the Agentic and Communal Properties of the Servant Leadership Questionnaire." *Journal of Leadership Education* 9.2 (2010): 4–21.

Barbuto, J. E. and D. W. Wheeler, "Scale Development and Construct Clarification of Servant Leadership." *Group & Organization Management* 31.3 (2006): 300–26.

Bennis, W. G., "Leadership Theory and Administrative Behavior: The Problem of Authority." *Administrative Science Quarterly* 4 (1959): 259–301. Doi:10.2307/2390911. Quoted in A. H. Eagly and J. Antonakis, "Leadership." Chapter 18, 571–592 in *APA Handbook of Personality and Social Psychology, Vol. 1. Attitudes and Social Cognition.* M. Mikulincer and P. R. Shaver, editors-in-chief. Washington, DC: American Psychological Association, 2015.

Bible, New International Version. Gospel of Mark. Gospel of John.

Bohnet, I., *What Works: Gender Equality by Design.* Cambridge, MA: Harvard University Press, 2016.

Chappel, D., "*Fortune*'s 'Best Companies to Work For' Embrace Servant Leadership." *The Servant Leader* 5 (2000), n.p.

Eagly, A. H. and L. L. Carli, *Through the Labyrinth: The Truth about How Women Become Leaders.* Boston: Harvard Business School Press, 2007.

Eagly, A. H. and M. C. Johannesen-Schmidt, "The Leadership Styles of Women and Men." *Journal of Social Issues* 57.4 (2001): 781–797.

Eagly, A. H. and S. J. Karau, "Role Congruity Theory of Prejudice toward Female Leaders." *Psychological Review* 109.3 (2002): 573–598.

Eicher-Catt, D., "The Myth of Servant-leadership: A Feminist Perspective." *Women and Language* 28.1 (2005): 17–25.

Germano, M., "Leadership and Value Co-Creation in Academic Libraries." In *Leadership in Academic Libraries Today: Connecting Theory to Practice*, edited by B. L. Eden and J. C Fagan. Lanham, MD: Rowman & Littlefield, 2014.

Gilligan, C., *In a Different Voice*. Cambridge, MA: Harvard University Press, 1982.

Graham, J. W., "Servant-leadership in Organizations: Inspirational and Moral." *Leadership Quarterly* 2.2 (1991): 105–119.

Greenleaf, R. K., *The Servant as Leader*. Cambridge, MA: Center for Applied Studies, 1970.

Harris, R. M., *Librarianship: The Erosion of a Woman's Profession*. Norwood, NJ: Ablex, 1992.

Hesse, H., *The Journey to the East*, translated by H. Rosner. New York: Farrar, Straus and Giroux, 1968.

Johnson, S. K., S. E. Murphy, S. Zewski, and R. J. Reichard, "The Strong Sensitive Type: Effects of Gender Stereotypes and Leader Prototypes on the Evaluation of Male and Female Leaders." *Organizational Behavior and Human Decision Processes* 106.1 (2008): 39–60.

Joseph, E. E. and B. E. Winston, "A Correlation of Servant Leadership, Leader Trust, and Organizational Trust." *Leadership & Organizational Development Journal* 26.1/2 (2005): 6–22.

Katopol, P., "Everybody Wins: Servant-Leadership." *Library Leadership & Management* 29.4 (2015): 1–7.

Laub, J. A., "Assessing the Servant Organization: Development of the Servant Organizational Leadership Assessment (SOLA) Instrument." PhD diss., Florida Atlantic University, 1999. Retrieved from Dissertations and Theses Fulltext. (AAT 9921922).

Liden, R. C., S. J. Wayne, H. Zhao, and D. Henderson, "Servant
Leadership: Development of a Multidimensional Measure
and Multi-level Assessment." *Leadership Quarterly* 19.2
(2008): 161–177.

Lowe, J. "Trust: The Invaluable Asset." In *Insights on Leadership*, edited
by L. C. Spears, 68–76. New York: Wiley, 1998.

Malenfant, K. J., "Understanding Faculty Perceptions of the Future:
Action Research for Academic Librarians." PhD diss., Antioch
University, 2011. Retrieved from http://aura.antioch.edu/etds/19/

Mayer, D. M., M. Bardes, and R. F. Piccolo, "Do Servant-leaders Help
Satisfy Follower Needs? An Organizational Justice Perspective."
European Journal of Work and Organizational Psychology 17.2
(2008): 180–197.

Meuser, J. D., R. C. Liden, S. J. Wayne, and D. J. Henderson, "Is
Servant Leadership Always a Good Thing? The Moderating
Influence of Servant Leadership Prototype." Paper presented at
the meeting of the Academy of Management, San Antonio, Texas,
August 2011.

Moniz, R., J. Henry, and J. Eshleman, *Fundamentals of the Academic
Library Liaison.* Chicago: Neil-Schuman/ALA, 2014.

Northouse, P. G., *Leadership: Theory and Practice*, 6th ed. Los Angeles:
Sage, 2013.

Project Implicit, Implicit Association Test. Retrieved from implicit.
harvard.edu.

Sendjaya, S. and J. C. Sarros, "Servant Leadership: Its Origin,
Development, and Application in Organizations." *Journal of
Leadership & Organizational Studies* 9.2 (2002): 57–64.

Smith, B. N., R. V. Montagno, and T. N. Kuzmenko,
"Transformational and Servant Leadership: Context and
Contextual Comparisons." *Journal of Leadership & Organizational
Studies* 10.4 (2004): 80–91.

Spears, L. C., ed. *Reflections on Leadership: How Robert K. Greenleaf's
Theory of Servant-leadership Influenced Today's Top Management
Thinkers.* New York: Wiley, 1995.

Spears, L. C. and M. Lawrence, eds. *Focus on Leadership: Servant-leadership for the Twenty-first Century.* New York: Wiley, 2002.

Weber, Max. "Politics as a Vocation" and "The Sociology of Charismatic Authority." In *From Max Weber: Essays in Sociology,* translated and edited by H. H. Gerth and C. Wright Mills. New York: Oxford University Press, 1946.

Embracing the Feminization of Librarianship

Shana Higgins

The piece of writing that got me thinking more deeply about the feminization of librarianship appears to have little if anything to do with gender: it was an article in the *Library Journal* by Rick Anderson.[1] And yet, I think it is very much about gendered, as well as other *Othering* anxieties in librarianship. In the spring of 2015 I had the opportunity to join five faculty members at my university in a multi-disciplinary seminar focused on gender, creativity and change.[2] This seminar allowed me to put the Anderson article into conversation with several other texts, including Melodie Fox and Hope Olson's chapter, "Essentialism and Care in a Female-Intensive Profession."[3] I presented provisional thoughts in relation to these analyses at the *Gender and Sexuality in Information Studies Colloquium* in Vancouver,

---

1 Rick Anderson, "Interrogating the American Library Association's 'Core Values' Statement," *Library Journal*, January 31, 2013, http://lj.libraryjournal.com/2013/01/opinion/peer-to-peer-review/interrogating-the-american-library-associations-core-values-statement-peer-to-peer-review/.

2 I owe gratitude to my colleagues at University of Redlands for introducing ideas that helped to germinate this chapter: Kathleen Feeley, Dorene Isenberg, Victoria Lewis, Jennifer Nelson, and Pauline Reynolds. And, as always, my thanks to Lua Gregory.

3 Melodie Fox, and Hope Olson,"Essentialism and Care in a Female-Intensive Profession," in *Feminist and Queer Information Studies Reader*, eds. Patrick Keilty and Rebecca Dean (Sacramento, CA: Litwin Books, 2013), 48-61.

April 2016.[4] The reading and writing that went into the following chapter provided an opportunity to continue to explore "embracing" our feminized labor as librarians.

TROUBLESOME "CORE VALUES"

In 2013 the *Library Journal* published Rick Anderson's article titled, "Interrogating the American Library Association's 'Core Values' Statement," in which Anderson parses what he determines as "internal contradictions" generated from the inclusion of "questionable 'core values'."[5] The "Core Values of Librarianship" statement summarizes the essential values of "modern librarianship" as expressed in a variety of key documents published by the American Library Association (ALA), including the *Library Bill of Rights*, the *Freedom to Read* statement, *Libraries: An American Value* statement, and are codified in the *ALA Policy Manual*.[6] Distilling and articulating a set of values at the core of the professional identities of a broad and varied profession must have been an arduous task, taken on by consecutive Task Force on Core Values groups in 1999 and 2004. In their recent special issue of *Library Trends*, editors Selinda A. Berg and Heidi LM Jacobs wrote that despite the problematic nature of attempting to reflect "what values were at the core of an incredibly diverse profession made up of a wide array of types of professional librarians who serve even more diverse populations of users"[7] the "Core Values" statement provides a touchstone for "[c]onversations about the values that provide the framework for librarian's work as individuals, as institutions, and as a profession [that] are critical to highlight both our points of convergence and points of divergence."[8] Herein I highlight some points of divergence.

---

4 Many thanks to the organizers Emily Drabinski, Tara Robertson, and Baharak Yousefi and to sponsor Rory Litwin.

5 Anderson, "Interrogating."

6 American Library Association, "Core Values of Librarianship," June 29, 2004, http://www.ala.org/advocacy/intfreedom/statementspols/corevalues.

7 Selinda A. Berg and Heidi LM Jacobs, "Introduction: Valuing Librarianship: Core Values in Theory and Practice," *Library Trends* 64, no. 3 (2016): 460. https://muse.jhu.edu/

8 Ibid., 462.

In his *Library Journal* article, Anderson wrote that *Access, Intellectual Freedom,* and *Service* were the primary "Core Values" whereas *Democracy, Education and Lifelong Learning, Social Responsibility,* and *The Public Good* were amongst the troublesome, conflicting "Core Values." In trying to process my indignation in relation to his claims I came to the conclusion that his argument reflected a particular dominant positionality that assumes a universal perspective and is situated in gendered discourses on library, information, and knowledge work. What if we examine the "Core Values" statement from the opposite perspective from which Anderson makes his claims? Those "Core Values" that Anderson considers inessential are, from an alternative perspective, that which drives librarianship, and to which all other "Core Values" are subordinate, or rather, from which they draw meaning? Would this reconceptualization orient our practices as library and information (LIS) professionals toward significantly reconsidered ethics of service and of access?[9]

Furthermore, the arguments that Anderson uses to discredit the "Core Values" of *Social Responsibility* and *The Public Good* might also be used to question *Access* and *Service* as possibly empty signifiers: Anderson suggests that the concepts of "'social responsibility' [and 'the public good'] without an agenda [are] meaningless."[10] Perhaps true. But it is equally valid to suggest that the values of *Access* and *Service* are meaningless without an agenda. What drives us to provide access and services in libraries? Commercial, for-profit entities can and do provide the kinds of access and services that libraries do— for a fee, generally, or, a cost of some sort. Libraries provide access and services for fundamentally different purposes that are contingent on understanding library work as framed by commitments to social responsibility and that are situated in particular communities.

Anderson's emphasis on access and service is common in librarianship. Whether explicitly, implicitly, primarily, or tangentially, a significant amount of literature in and about LIS focuses on issues of access and providing service(s), yet access and services are rarely challenged or examined as the central tenets of our profession. I

---

9 Gabrielle Dean, "The Shock of the Familiar: Three Timelines about Gender and Technology in the Library," *Digital Humanities Quarterly* 9, no. 2 (2015). http://www.digitalhumanities.org/dhq/vol/9/2/000201/000201.html

10 Anderson, "Interrogating."

will argue that this emphasis, to the exclusion of other professional values, is deeply wound in the gendered discourses of librarianship. As a response, I will explore the ways in which the feminine-coded qualities of librarianship and the "feminization" of library work may be aligned with (re)asserting an agenda for libraries that builds from a foundation of serving the public good and of social responsibility.

OUR FEMINIZED LABOR

Most readers of this chapter are likely aware that librarianship in North America has been a predominantly white, female workforce, at least since the late 19th Century.[11] In part we can thank Melvil Dewey for this. Dewey founded the School of Library Economy at Columbia College in 1887, admitting and actively recruiting women, and with a firm belief that women were well suited to library work: "The natural qualities most important in library work…are accuracy, order (or what we call the housekeeping instinct), executive ability, and above all earnestness and enthusiasm."[12] Likewise John Cotton Dana, a Dewey contemporary and supporter, described women's natural affinity for library work along the lines of "conventional stereotypes of the ideal woman as pleasant, malleable, helpful, accurate, detail-oriented, naturally intuitive, but not too smart."[13] Dewey, and others, also recognized women as more economical, requiring lower wages. Limited opportunities for educated women, coupled with a willingness to conform or concede to feminine stereotypes, led to the lower paid, lower status workforce and profession. Not only did librarianship become, and has remained, female intensive, but also library work became characterized as 'feminine.' Feminized professions—including nursing, social work, and paralegals—are predominantly service-, support- and care-oriented, and often require more intensive affective labor. As opposed to masculine-coded

---

11 Dee Garrison, *Apostles of Culture: The Public Librarian and American Society, 1876-1920* (New York: Macmillan Information, 1979); Abigail A. Van Slyck, *Free to All: Carnegie Libraries & American Culture, 1890-1920* (Chicago: University of Chicago Press, 1995) and Gina Schlesselman-Tarango, "The Legacy of Lady Bountiful: White Women in the Library," *Library Trends* 64, no. 4 (2016). doi:10.1353/lib.2016.0015.

12 Van Slyck, *Free to All*, 163.

13 Ibid., 165.

productive labor, whether that is making and building, requiring increased education and expertise, or simply defined as productive based on wage scales. Roxanne Shirazi has suggested that academic librarianship can be seen as the reproductive labor of the academy, supporting the productive labor of research and scholarship.[14] It is also useful to recognize that women's work, or more broadly feminized labor, is often invisible. Care, maintenance, and service work done well are seamless in such a way as to be invisible, and often take place in private spaces. Here I highlight the correspondence between care work that takes place behind closed doors, whether in the home or institution, and maintenance work that may or may not take place behind closed doors, such as janitorial work, work visa processing, and copy cataloging.

This only scratches the surface of productive versus reproductive labor discourses, leaving out much, including intersectional experiences of feminized work. Feminized, reproductive and maintenance work are as much about class, ethnicity and race as they are about gender. Miere Laderman Ukeles' late 1960s and 1970s photographic and performance art work on "care" and "maintenance art" drew attention to the parallels between the nearly invisible work of care and maintenance.[15] A 1974 photograph titled *Transfer: The Maintenance of the Art Object* is a portrait of the artist, a white woman, a museum conservator, a brown man, and a custodian, a white man.[16] In the black and white photograph, both men wear uniforms, Ukeles does not and wears all white, thus calling attention to their difference and signifying a lower social status of the men in uniform. In the parallel performance piece Ukeles cleans the protective display case for a piece of art work, naming this work "dust painting." Once the work has been defined as "art" the responsibility for the cleaning be-

---

14 Shirazi makes this claim specifically in the context of digital humanities work. Roxanne Shirazi, "Reproducing the Academy: Librarians and the Question of Service in the Digital Humanities," July 15, 2014, accessed February 2, 2016. http://roxanneshirazi.com/2014/07/15/reproducing-the-academy-librarians-and-the-question-of-service-in-the-digital-humanities/.

15 Miere Ukeles, "Manifesto for Maintenance Art, 1969! Proposal for an Exhibition 'Care.'" accessed February 10, 2016. http://www.feldmangallery.com/media/pdfs/Ukeles_MANIFESTO.pdf.

16 Miere Ukeles, "Transfer: The Maintenance of the Art Object." http://www.learn.columbia.edu/courses/fa/images/large/kc_femart_ukeles_79.jpg

comes that of an art conservator. The same work—cleaning a display case—is transformed when performed by a custodian, an artist, or an art conservator. "Ukeles's role as 'artist' allowed her to reconfigure the value bestowed upon these otherwise unobtrusive maintenance operations, and to explore the ramifications of making maintenance labor visible in public."[17] In the photograph, Ukeles makes visible the intersection of class, ethnicity and race, and gender. In her *Manifesto for Maintenance Art, 1969! Proposal for an exhibition "CARE,"* Ukeles divides work into the categories of development and maintenance, a parallel to productive and reproductive labor.

> *Two basic systems: Development and Maintenance. The sourball of*
> *every revolution: after the revolution, who's going*
> *to pick up the garbage on Monday morning?*
>
> *Development: pure individual creation; the new; change; progress;*
> *advance; excitement; flight or fleeing.*
>
> *Maintenance: keep the dust off the pure individual creation;*
> *preserve the new; sustain the change; protect progress; defend*
> *and prolong the advance; renew the excitement; repeat the*
> *flight; show your work—show it again*
> *keep the contemporaryartmuseum groovy keep the home*
> *fires burning*
>
> *Development systems are partial feedback systems with major room*
> *for change.*
>
> *Maintenance systems are direct feedback systems with little room for*
> *alteration.*[18]

Ukeles' photographic and performance art limned cultural understandings of male-coded and female-coded work, as well as classed and racialized work. Likewise her work drew connections between the gendered, classed, and racialized labor of care, service, and support work. All of which linger today.

---

17 Helen Molesworth, "House Work and Art Work." *October* 92 (2000): 71-97.

18 Ukeles, "Manifesto for Maintenance Art."

FEMINIST CONCEPTIONS OF AN ETHICS OF CARE

In trying to think through my own and others' ideas in relation to gendered conceptions of our values in librarianship, as a female intensive-profession, I found myself back in the 1970s and 1980s. Both the multi-disciplinary seminar in which I participated and reading Victoria Hesford's *Feeling Women's Liberation* prompted me to reflect on what may have been lost in the break from second-wave feminism that could be useful in imagining more equitable futures in LIS.[19] Care seems to hold possibilities as a means toward equitable, inclusive, anti-neoliberal futures. Second-wave feminist scholars have grappled with and advocated an ethics of care that is deeply connected to women's ways of being and knowing. Carol Gilligan "claimed that on the average, and for a variety of cultural reasons, women tend to espouse an ethics of care that stresses relationships and responsibilities, whereas men tend to espouse an ethics of justice that stresses rules and rights."[20] For some feminists, myself included, an ethics of care has felt too close to essentialist conceptions of our sexed and gendered selves. Writing in response to such critics, Gilligan made clear that she considers the "care perspective…neither biologically determined nor unique to women."[21] Eva Kittay makes a similar fine distinction in her formulation of a "feminist public ethic of care."[22] Care work, or what she calls "dependency work," has been predominantly women's work, and most especially poor women's work through its alignment with traditional patriarchal and hetero-normative notions of gendered labor within familial structures. Kittay argues that recognizing "dependency work" as legitimate and vital to the well-being of society may result in "possibilities for well-being of individuals and for justice within collectivities [to] proliferate in as yet unimagined ways."[23]

---

19 Victoria Hesford, *Feeling Women's Liberation* (Durham, NC: Duke University Press, 2013).

20 Rosemary Tong, "Carol Gilligan's Ethics of Care," in *Feminine and Feminist Ethics* (Belmont, CA: Wadsworth Publishing Companing, 1993), 80.

21 Carol Gilligan, "Reply to Critics," in *An Ethic of Care*, ed. Mary J. Larrabee (New York : Routledge, 1993), 209.

22 Eva Feder Kittay, "A Feminist Public Ethic of Care Meets the New Communitarian Family Policy," *Ethics* 111, no. 3 (2001): 523-547.

23 Ibid., 547.

The public aspect of Kittay's care ethic identifies care as not solely about intimate relations and private spaces, but rather challenges us to see the multiple "nested dependencies" in which we live, the public domain included.[24]

Patricia Hill Collins recognized a connection between an ethic of care rooted in women's experience and "Afrocentric expressions of the ethic of caring."[25] For Collins there are three components to an ethic of caring within the African American community: "the value placed on individual expressiveness, the appropriateness of emotions, and the capacity for empathy."[26] Furthermore, Collins suggests that the value placed by African American communities on "individual uniqueness, personal expressiveness, and empathy" is correlative to feminist emphasis on "women's 'inner voice'."[27] The "inner voice" refers to subjective knowledge, and a recognition of one's self as an authority. While Collins distinguished an Afrocentric feminist ethic of care from an "abstract, unemotional Western masculinity,"[28] Mary Belenky and colleagues theorized the concept of women's "inner voice," or subjective knowledge, as an alternative to a similar masculine ideal of disembodied, rights-based epistemology.[29] In other words, Gilligan, Kittay, Collins, Belenky, amongst others tried to theorize a capacity for care, an epistemology anchored by care and empathy, that may develop from lived and/or shared experiences of oppression and marginalization, and those tasked with responsibility for the well-being of others.

24 Eva Feder Kittay, "The Ethics of Care, Dependency, and Disability," *Ratio Juris* 24, no. 1 (2011): 49-58.

25 Patricia Hill Collins, "The Social Construction of Black Feminist Thought," *Signs: Journal of Women in Culture and Society* 14, no. 4 (1989): 767.

26 Ibid., 767.

27 Patrcia Hill Collins, *Black Feminist Thought* (New York, NY: Routledge Classics, 2009), 283.

28 Collins, "The Social Construction of Black Feminist Thought," 767.

29 Mary Belenky, *Women's Ways of Knowing: The Development of Self, Voice, and Mind* (New York: Basic Books, 1986).

AN ETHIC OF CARE IN LIS

In the early 1990s Roma M. Harris, Jane A. Hannigan, and Hilary Crew published work that examined librarianship through a feminist lens. Harris's book, *Librarianship: The Erosion of a Woman's Profession*,[30] covered a range of issues including women's status in the profession, cultural representations of librarians, and the role of the American Library Association in librarianship. While Harris does not explicitly address a care ethic, she did argue "for preserving values of librarianship as a female-intensive profession by resisting the privatization of services and the drive toward professionalization," instead suggesting that we re-embrace "the old librarianship by restoring to it a brand of female professionalism."[31] Hannigan and Crew proposed a new model of research and scholarship for LIS that draws on the female-intensive nature of librarianship, one that is "cooperative, participatory, interdisciplinary, and nonhierarchical... thereby becoming an exemplar of the very things it promotes."[32] Hannigan and Crew argued that a feminist model of scholarship would be relational, or that which incorporates an ethic of care, and can be epistemologically categorized as *constructed knowledge*. Hannigan and Crew define *constructed knowledge* as emphasizing interdependence and contexuality.[33] These emphases on cooperativeness, interdependence, and contextuality as specific to a female-intensive profession, or space, are well aligned with feminist theories of care ethics of the same time period.

In the past few years the concept of care has re-emerged. It seems fitting that an ethic of care has also made a return in the female-intensive profession of librarianship. In *Feminist Pedagogy for Library Instruction*, Maria T. Accardi associates feminist teaching practice with caring about and caring for students. Through the work of Nel Noddings, Accardi connects a gendered ethical orientation toward caring with feminist practice, one that values personal and individual

---

30 Roma M. Harris, *Librarianship: The Erosion of a Woman's Profession* (Norwood, NJ: Ablex Pub., 1992).

31 Ibid., 163.

32 Jane Hannigan and Hilary Crew, "A Feminist Paradigm for Library and Information Science," *Wilson Library Bulletin*, October, 1993: 28.

33 Hannigan and Crew, "A Feminist Paradigm for Library and Information Science," 30.

experiences, affirms and nurtures, and develops trust. While these values have historically been considered the domain of women's experience, Accardi notes that Noddings refers to "relational ethics" as a means to de-gender or de-essentialize an ethical orientation toward caring.[34] Relational theory suggests that the self is constituted through our relationships with others as opposed to the self being formed by a set of universal values. Relational ethics means that decisions and actions are made within the context of a relationship or set of relationships, are based on mutual respect and willingness to understand the unique situation of an individual or group, and make use of both our intellectual as well as emotional abilities. Beth Nowviskie, writing on capacity and care in the digital humanities, draws on Noddings's conception of "engrossment." Engrossment is a "kind of close attention and focus on the other" that leads to empathy, or specifically a "productive appreciation of the standpoint or position of that person or group."[35] Accardi and Nowviskie limn a similar aspect of Noddings's concept of care: that which is receptive and responsive to the cared-for.[36] Michelle Caswell and Marika Cifor, in relation to archival practices, suggest "radical empathy" as an approach that "assumes that subjects are embodied, that we are inextricably bound to each other through relationships, that we live in complex relations to each other infused with power differences and inequities, and that we care about each other's well-being."[37] A significant aspect of the radical empathy they posit is that it recognizes difference; it does not blur "the lines between self and other."[38]

In their chapter, "Essentialism and Care in a Female-Intensive Profession," Fox and Olson trace some of the feminist debates in relation to an ethics of care rooted in women's experience, specifically in relation to the work of Carol Gilligan and Gayatri Spivak. In doing

---

34 Maria T. Accardi, *Feminist Pedagogy for Library Instruction* (Sacramento, CA: Library Juice Press, 2013): 44-45.

35 Beth Nowviskie, "On Capacity and Care," *Nowviskie.org*, October 4, 2015, http://nowviskie.org/2015/on-capacity-and-care/.

36 Nel Noddings, "Caring in Education," *The Encyclopedia of Informal Education*, 2005, http://infed.org/mobi/caring-in-education/.

37 Michelle Caswell and Marika Cifor, "From Human Rights to Feminist Ethics: Radical Empathy in the Archives," *Archivaria* 81, (Spring 2016): 31.

38 Ibid., 31.

so they illuminate the impetus for feminist developments of an ethic of care. Second-wave feminists were interested in conceptualizing a situated ethics, a contextualized sense of justice and responsibility in opposition, or perhaps complimentary, to a rigid set of rights and universal rules—a Rawlsian sense of justice characterized as masculine. A Rawlsian theory (John Rawls) of justice has been criticized by feminists for centering the individual—over the public good—and economic liberty over other forms of well-being. In relation to libraries, Fox and Olson write that "an ethic of care seems logical and right, given libraries' social mission...An ethic of care includes willingness to hear another perspective, deeper delving to get at context, and bending of rules to endeavor to satisfy any user's need."[39] Their chapter culminates with the question, "Can librarianship take advantage of its female-intensiveness to assert an ethic of care in our practice?"[40]

CARE ETHIC AND STANDPOINT THEORY

"Feminist thought is forced to 'speak as' and on behalf of the very notion it criticizes and tries to dismantle—women. In the contradictory nature of this project lies both its greatest challenge and a source of its great creativity."[41]

There are affinities, and perhaps genealogical relations, between theorizations of an ethic of care and of standpoint theory. As with a care ethic, standpoint theory centers non-dominant and marginalized perspectives and lived experiences. Likewise, standpoint theory claims all knowledge and ways of knowing are socially situated. According to Sandra Harding, standpoint theory produces a new subject of knowledge, one differentiated from the subject of empiricist knowledge. This new subject is culturally and historically situated, as are the objects of knowledge, and that this knowledge is produced and legitimated by communities, rather than individuals. Finally, the subjects of knowledge from a feminist

---

39 Fox and Olson. "Essentialism and Care in a Female-Intensive Profession," 58.

40 Ibid.

41 Sandra Harding, "Rethinking Standpoint Epistemology," in *Feminist Epistemologies*, eds. Linda Alcoff and Elizabeth Potter, (New York: Routledge, 1993): 49-82.

standpoint theory are "multiple, heterogeneous, and contradictory or incoherent, not unitary, homogeneous, and coherent as they are for empiricist epistemology."[42]

Sara Ahmed notes that a "central thesis of standpoint feminism [is] that the experience of oppression has epistemic significance."[43] In other words, one's lived experience of oppression and marginalization necessarily affects one's world-making. Yet, the relationship between experience and knowledge is not so simple. Feminist standpoint theories are complex in related ways to feminist conceptions of an ethic of care. Harding argues that a standpoint is not merely a perspective; standpoints are socially, politically, scientifically mediated, whereas, according to Harding, perspectives are unmediated. Thus, "the logic of standpoint approaches contains within it both an essentializing tendency and also resources to combat such a tendency. Feminist standpoint theory is not in itself either essentialist or nonessentialist, racist or antiracist, ethnocentric or not. It contains tendencies in each direction, it contains contradictions."[44] Furthermore in standpoint theories, our selves are contradictory insofar as we become "subjects and generators of thought, not just objects of others' thoughts."[45] Harding explains that to be a female scientist or an African American philosopher is to "think and act out of contradictory social locations," both dominant and non-dominant.[46] Like feminist conceptions of an ethic of care, feminist standpoints inhabit potentially regressive essentializing as well as liberatory spaces. Feminist standpoint theory and feminist care ethics also share an imperative to start from the stance of the marginalized, the othered, as a means to bring those ways of being and knowing to the center.

---

42 Harding, "Rethinking Standpoint Epistemology," 65.

43 Sara Ahmed, *On Being Included: Racism and Diversity in Institutional Life*, (Durham: Duke University Press, 2012): 217.

44 Sandra Harding, *Whose Science? Whose Knowledge?: Thinking from Women's Lives*, (Ithaca, NY: Cornell University Press, 1991): 180.

45 Ibid., 275.

46 Ibid., 275.

BACK TO LANGUAGE: GENDERING ACCESS AND SERVICES

In theorizing an alternative conception of justice via an ethic of care, feminists have defined a set of relational values that distinguish a care ethic from a Western, masculine sense of justice. They do so in purposefully feminine and masculine coded language. See the table below for an enumeration of some of these feminine- and masculine-coded values.

Feminine-Coded	Masculine-Coded
relationships	rules
responsibilities	rights
situational	abstract
empathy	unemotional
expressiveness	individual
community	economic liberty
subjective	objective
unique	universal
heterogeneous	homogeneous

Collins calls attention to the value placed on "individual uniqueness" and "personal expressiveness" in African American communities. How does this differ from a Eurocentric, masculinist emphasis on the individual? Claiming a unique perspective, developed through one's lived experience is to also acknowledge that the self is always forged in relation to others. Our lived experiences are shaped via their connectedness to others' experiences. In contrast, individuality is most often conceptualized as being separate and independent of others, as if born to the world fully formed without interference from others.

Reading Anderson's article, "Interrogating the American Library Association's 'Core Values,'" again, it becomes clear to me that his understanding of the "Core Values" is gendered, reflecting a Western, masculinist, and seemingly universal perspective. Anderson asks, "What are the deepest and most basic purposes of the library?" For Anderson these are providing access with service, and supporting intellectual freedom. According to Anderson, *Access* is the Library's primary function, and more important than collections, "because collections exist for the purpose of supporting access, not the other way around."[47] Certainly the ethos of libraries is to provide freely available access to information (collections). However, preservation of collections of materials may not always be in the immediate service of access. Preservation of artifacts from marginalized or precarious communities and organizations serving those communities may require limited access, at least in the short term. I am in agreement with Anderson in relation to the importance of service, without which a library would be "a collection of documents sitting in a building." Anderson's hyperbole risks regressively suggesting that libraries are simply warehouses of print materials. Nonetheless libraries are services—supplying a public need, a public good—and they provide services—maintaining systems of access, developing and maintaining systems of discovery—and library workers engage in service-oriented activities—providing aid, instruction, and in the best cases, being of use to their communities. Anderson's understanding of *Intellectual Freedom* as a "Core Value" is mechanistically oriented, with a focus on the structures that "enhance" and "restrict" access. As examples, Anderson highlights borrowing time limits as the structure that enhances access, the structure that enables the greatest number of people to have access to a resource, and vaguely alludes to restrictions on access for materials that some patrons might find offensive. Anderson further elaborates on intellectual freedom and access in a scenario in which "two core values come into conflict," the "subordinate" core value, privacy, and the "fundamental" core values, access and intellectual freedom.[48] In this scenario, a colleague questions offering access to a resource that requires the provision of personal information in order to use. For this colleague the requirement to provide personal information "constitute[s] a breach of the patron's privacy."[49] For Anderson, to withhold access to this resource would mean that the library/librarians were impinging on the intellectual freedom rights of patrons. Anderson's scenario is an either/or situation: "when two core values come into conflict, you

---

47 Anderson, "Interrogating."

48 Ibid.

49 Ibid.

need a way of deciding which one will win."[50] Anderson chooses to ignore the ways in which a right to privacy and intellectual freedom are deeply embedded in the other. "When users recognize or fear that their privacy or confidentiality is compromised, true freedom of inquiry no longer exists."[51] By describing this situation as a conflict, as either/or, in which one core value trumps the other, Anderson appeals to masculine-coded concepts of rules and rights that must be universally applied. In contrast, the *Library Bill of Rights* describes the relationship between privacy/confidentiality and intellectual freedom in which patrons have the right to be informed in order to make choices. Thus, the *Library Bill of Rights* already leans toward an ethic of care, one more aligned with feminine-coded values, insofar as it emphasizes the heterogeneity of our patrons, their agency to make situational decisions, and the responsibilities of the library/librarians to contribute to informed decisions.

Anderson closes his article with the "questionable 'Core Values,'" although he finds nothing "bad or wrong in and of themselves,"[52] Anderson questions how we can simultaneously hold democracy, diversity, and intellectual freedom as core values of librarianship given that these concepts ostensibly contradict. If valuing diversity, he argues, means serving patrons with anti-democratic ideals, how can we claim democracy—defined as political philosophy—as a professional value? Anderson's definition of democracy in this article differs from that in the ALA statement, in which the emphasis is on supporting an informed citizenry.[53] One can also choose to define democracy in relation to a belief in social equality. Each of these perspectives on the concept of democracy is political in nature, but Anderson adheres to a rules-based and singular notion of democracy. Likewise, the primary concern Anderson has with social responsibility and the concept of the public good is that we have no universal, homogeneous definition of what these mean or how to enact them. Finally, Anderson questions *Education and Lifelong Learning* as a "Core Value" by harkening

---

50 Ibid.

51 American Library Association, "Privacy," July 1, 2004, http://www.ala.org/advocacy/intfreedom/librarybill/interpretations/privacy

52 Ibid.

53 American Library Association, "Core Values of Librarianship," June 29, 2004, http://www.ala.org/advocacy/intfreedom/statementspols/corevalues.

back to an elitist notion that "recreational resources" have little educational value.[54]

Reading Anderson's interrogation of the "Core Values" from a feminist standpoint, I see a Eurocentric, masculinist version of the values of librarianship emerge, one that seeks to define our values as universal, objective, and neutral rather than embracing the heterogeneity and context of the communities we serve, nor comfortable with defining our service according to our responsibilities to and relationships with our communities. A feminist standpoint toward the "Core Values" would center *Social Responsibility* and *The Public Good* as the values that drive and inform the ways in which access to collections, information, spaces, and services are provided.

The feminine as resistance

Rather than enforcing notions of women's "natural" predisposition toward care and nurturing, many feminist scholars have negotiated the connections of an ethic of care with lived experience. All of them informed by their experiences as women: for Collins, the intersectional experience as a Black woman; for Kittay, the experience of a woman and mother of a child living with a disability; and for Fox and Olson, as women in a female-intensive profession. However, lived experience is merely a condition that *may* foster adopting an ethic of care. A feminist ethic of care is also a strategic choice. Reading Teresa de Lauretis's "The Essence of the Triangle," Victoria Hesford writes that for de Lauretis, taking the "risk of essentialism" is "less an assertion of some natural innate being-ness of women and more...a potentiality, a radical project of reimagining the social and cultural domains—a reimagining that is part of the process of constituting 'new social spaces' and 'new forms of community'."[55] In claiming the feminine we can enact a different "symbolization, a different production of reference and meaning out of a particular embodied knowledge."[56] In

---

54 Anderson, "Interrogating."

55 Victoria Hesford, *Feeling Women's Liberation* (Durham, NC: Duke University Press, 2013): 243.

56 Teresa de Lauretis, "The Essence of the Triangle, or Taking the Risk of Essentialism Seriously: Feminist Theory in Italy, the U.S, and Britain," *differences: A Journal of Feminist Cultural Studies* 1, no. 2 (Summer 1989):27.

what I think is a complementary claim, Collins suggests that "using an Afrocentric feminist epistemology calls into question the content of what currently passes as truth and simultaneously challenges the process of arriving at that truth."[57]

I would like for our profession to harness these radical desires and ideas to form "new social spaces" and challenge the processes of arriving at truths in our profession. I'd like to answer Fox and Olson's question with an affirmative, that we can take the "risk of essentialism" as de Lauretis puts it, as well as the risk of the continued "symbolic feminine" or feminization of our profession. As library workers we need not engage in acts of nurturing, but in the way that we structure our spaces, services, and programs we can draw on our capacity to empathize, and be sensitive to the affective qualities of our work. Regardless of our sexed and gendered bodies, and of our gender identities, we can reclaim our feminized labor as practicing feminism. A feminist care ethic may enable us to center the collaborative, communal, and politically engaged-ness of library work. And thus the "Core Values" most relevant and strategic to library work would include *Social Responsibility* and *The Public Good*. These become the reasons why we provide access—and accessibility—and provide services.

In the process of subverting our current "truths" we might also redefine service and access in our work. Gabrielle Dean has argued that over time, service in librarianship has not only accrued the subservient meaning of our feminized work but we've also allowed an elision of service and services, and of human and machine.[58] Likewise, access has become more about expediency, heavily weighted toward the readily available, than about the "equitably accessible" piece of the "Core Values."

FROM CARE TO INTERDEPENDENCE

Those who have theorized and critiqued an ethic of care at the intersection of feminist, gender, and disability perspectives suggest the concept of interdependence. Interdependence could be a way to revalue our relationships and responsibilities both to our communities as well

---

57 Collins, "The Social Construction of Black Feminist Thought," 773.

58 Dean, "The Shock of the Familiar," 48-52.

as to and within our institutions.[59] The concept of interdependence allows us to recognize the limits of individualism, and the limits of single entities within institutions, while moving us "toward a politics in which we acknowledge our inevitable need for each other" in creating new possibilities through "collaborative resistance."[60] Of her activism Alicia Garza, co-founder of #BlackLivesMatter, says, "we are building a world that values interdependence, values collaboration and cooperation, and also values the unique experiences of people."[61] This sense of interdependence in the service of creating new social spaces coalesces many of the theoretical positions of second wave feminists—Patricia Hill Collins, Teresa de Lauretis, Eva Kittay, Sandra Harding, etc.—in recognizing difference within common cause. In 1989 de Lauretis asked if a future for feminism existed without confronting the "essential difference of feminism as socio-historical formation."[62] I think we risk the future of libraries if we choose not to embrace an intersectional feminist practice, a feminist practice that takes a different path than the hegemony of liberal feminism but instead embraces the heterogeneity of feminist practices while working toward common causes.

Perhaps an interdependence perspective would allow library workers (including leaders) to do several things that relate to care—for ourselves, for our communities, and for our administrators: make visible our affective, 'reproductive,' and maintenance work; increase and strengthen collaborative work with our communities, patrons, and users in all areas of library work; and enable us to move away from return-on-investment talk toward valuing "our inevitable need for each other"[63] within the institution. A significant amount of library work and library operations remain invisible to those unfamiliar with the complex, interconnected work that maintains the library.

---

59 When I write of communities and institutions it is from the perspective of an academic librarian within the structure of a university.

60 Kathryn Abrams, "Performing Interdependence: Judith Butler and Sunaura Taylor in the Examined Life." *Columbia Journal of Gender and Law* 21, no. 2 (2011), 89.

61 Sara Grossman, Q & A with Alicia Garza, co-creator of #BlackLivesMatter, April 15, 2015, http://conference.otheringandbelonging.org/blog/2015/4/25/qa-with-alicia-garza-co-creator-of-blacklivesmatter

62 De Lauretis, "The Essence of the Triangle," 33.

63 Abrams, "Performing Interdependence," 89.

Management of electronic resources, development and maintenance of systems, and even cataloging are mostly invisible to students and faculty across the university, as well as to administrators who make budgetary decisions that impact library operations and personnel. This invisible labor, and those who perform it, need colleagues and leaders who champion and make visible the significance of their work. We can illuminate this maintenance work in instructional settings, in advocacy and marketing, and in budget and planning conversations. Likewise, certain kinds of library work are devalued both within the library and across the institution. In my experience, technical positions, those that require more interaction with integrated library systems and associated hardware and software, have higher wages, even if still underpaid. Public services (access services) staff members who engage in more traditional affective labor—services with smiles—are viewed as providing unskilled labor. Skillfully determining the needs of students, faculty, staff, and administrators; knowledgeably referring those in need to appropriate individuals and services; and assisting in the navigation of the library's resources and services with expertise and abilities of an *empath* is valuable work, deserving equitable pay. Lisa Sloniowski, in her feminist analysis of academic librarian work and affective labor, draws attention to the division between techno-intellectual labor and emotional labor: "it may seem easy at first to distinguish between different librarian organizational silos, the reality is that our work deeply impacts and shapes one another…Nonetheless, certain forms of digital immaterial labor are valorized as mind work over the emotion work of liaison librarians, and such valorizations have their roots in gendered divisions of labor."[64] Similar divisions exist across roles and departments within an academic library. Yet academic libraries are capable of becoming small-scale exemplars of valuing interdependence, requiring the necessary marriage of affective and technical skills, social and maintenance abilities.

Deepening relationships between academic libraries and their varied communities holds the possibility of amplifying the value of interdependence, which in turn may be the means to resist neoliberal pressures to quantify return-on-investment for personnel, time, services, and other resources. Inviting student groups, faculty

---

64 Lisa Sloniowski, "Affective Labor, Resistance, and the Academic Librarian," *Library Trends* 64, no. 4 (2016): 653.

groups, and local community groups to partner with the library to develop programs and curate exhibits would address gaps in our collections and resources, and less than inclusive library spaces. Such partnerships make explicit interdependencies. It may be a stretch to imagine the academic library as akin to marginalized or subjugated communities and cultures. Yet we may feel marginal when we hear the not uncommon refrain from our colleagues in other university departments, "but everything is online now." For them the building, the physical collections, the maintenance of collections (digital, physical, and otherwise), the expertise and knowledge of librarians and library staff, are in need of repurposing and/or are redundant. Partnering with community groups who likewise feel marginalized, or socially devalued, creates a means to empower both those communities and the library. Such mutual care has the possibility of substantiating alternative value(s) and worldviews, and imagining, as Kittay suggested "possibilities for well-being of individuals and for justice within collectivities...in yet unimagined ways."[65]

What seems most urgent now is that we should practice a radical feminist ethics of care and practice from feminist standpoints in order to decenter dominant positionalities, bodies, systems, and perspectives in our work. In order to do this, we have to interrogate our positions and standpoints and question what we consider common sense or intuitive in our policies and processes. It would mean that libraries and library workers eschew the notion of neutrality[66] and work toward social justice goals that seek to dismantle patriarchal, white supremacist, Eurocentric, and hegemonic practices and systems that prevail in our profession.

---

65 Eva Feder Kittay, "A Feminist Public Ethic of Care Meets the New Communitarian Family Policy," *Ethics* 111, no. 3 (2001): 523-547.

66 Take a look at the activism, scholarship, and public intellectual work of Safiya Noble, Chris Bourg, April Hathcock, Emily Drabinski, Maura Seale, @ StorytimeUnderground, and many others for arguments against a position of neutrality in libraries.

BIBLIOGRAPHY

Abrams, Kathryn. "Performing Interdependence: Judith Butler and Sunaura Taylor in the Examined Life." *Columbia Journal of Gender and Law* 21, no. 2 (2011): 72-89.

Accardi, Maria T. *Feminist Pedagogy for Library Instruction.* Sacramento, CA: Library Juice Press, 2013.

Ahmed, Sara. *On Being Included: Racism and Inclusion Institutional Life.* Durham, NC: Duke University Press, 2012.

American Library Association. "Core Values of Librarianship." June 29, 2004, http://www.ala.org/advocacy/intfreedom/statementspols/corevalues.

American Library Association, "Privacy," July 1, 2004, http://www.ala.org/advocacy/intfreedom/librarybill/interpretations/privacy

Anderson, Rick. "Interrogating the American Library Association's 'Core Values' Statement," *Library Journal*, January 31, 2013. http://lj.libraryjournal.com/2013/01/opinion/peer-to-peer-review/interrogating-the-american-library-associations-core-values-statement-peer-to-peer-review/.

Belenky, Mary. *Women's Ways of Knowing: The Development of Self, Voice, and Mind.* New York: Basic Books, 1986.

Berg, Selinda A. and Heidi LM Jacobs. "Introduction: Valuing Librarianship: Core Values in Theory and Practice." *Library Trends* 64, no. 3 (2016): 459-467. https://muse.jhu.edu/.

Caswell, Michelle and Marika Cifor. "From Human Rights to Feminist Ethics: Radical Empathy in the Archives." *Archivaria* 81, (Spring 2016): 23-43.

Collins, Patricia Hill. "The Social Construction of Black Feminist Thought," *Signs: Journal of Women in Culture and Society* 14, no. 4 (1989): 745-773.

———. *Black Feminist Thought.* New York, NY: Routledge Classics, 2009.

Dean, Gabrielle. "The Shock of the Familiar: Three Timelines about Gender and Technology in the Library." *Digital Humanities Quarterly* 9, no. 2 (2015). http://www.digitalhumanities.org/dhq/vol/9/2/000201/000201.html.

De Lauretis, Teresa. "The Essence of the Triangle, or Taking the Risk of Essentialism Seriously: Feminist Theory in Italy, the U.S, and Britain." *differences: A Journal of Feminist Cultural Studies* 1, no. 2 (Summer 1989): 4-37.

Feder Kittay, Eva. "A Feminist Public Ethic of Care Meets the New Communitarian Family Policy." *Ethics* 111, no. 3 (2001): 523-547.

Fox, Melodie, and Hope Olson. "Essentialism and Care in a Female-Intensive Profession." In *Feminist and Queer Information Studies Reader*, edited by Patrick Keilty and Rebecca Dean, 48-61. Sacramento, CA: Litwin Books, 2013.

Garrison, Dee. *Apostles of Culture: The Public Librarian and American Society, 1876-1920.* New York: Macmillan Information, 1979.

Gilligan, Carol. "Reply to Critics." In *An Ethic of Care*, edited by Mary J. Larrabee, 207-214. New York : Routledge, 1993.

Grossman, Sara. "Q & A with Alicia Garza, co-creator of #BlackLivesMatter." April 15, 2015. http://conference.otheringandbelonging.org/blog/2015/4/25/qa-with-alicia-garza-co-creator-of-blacklivesmatter.

Hannigan, Jane and Hilary Crew. "A Feminist Paradigm for Library and Information Science." *Wilson Library Bulletin*, October, 1993: 28-32.

Harding, Sandra. "Rethinking Standpoint Epistemology." In *Feminist Epistemologies*, edited by Linda Alcoff and Elizabeth Potter,49-82. New York: Routledge, 1993.

Harding, Sandra. *Reinventing Ourselves as Other*. Ithaca, NY: Cornell University Press, 1991.

Harris, Roma M. *Librarianship: The Erosion of a Woman's Profession.* Norwood, NJ: Ablex Publishers, 1992.

Hesford, Victoria. *Feeling Women's Liberation*. Durham, NC: Duke University Press, 2013.

Molesworth, Helen. "House Work and Art Work." *October* 92 (2000): 71-97.

Noddings, Nel. "Caring in Education." *The Encyclopedia of Informal Education*, 2005. http://infed.org/mobi/caring-in-education/.

Nowviskie, Beth. "On Capacity and Care." *Nowviskie.org.* October 4, 2015. http://nowviskie.org/2015/on-capacity-and-care/.

Schlesselman-Tarango, Gina. "The Legacy of Lady Bountiful: White Women in the Library." *Library Trends* 64, no. 4 (2016). https://muse.jhu.edu/.

Shirazi, Roxanne. "Reproducing the Academy: Librarians and the Question of Service in the Digital Humanities." *roxanneshirazi.com.* July 15, 2014. http://roxanneshirazi.com/2014/07/15/reproducing-the-academy-librarians-and-the-question-of-service-in-the-digital-humanities/.

Sloniowski, Lisa. "Affective Labor, Resistance, and the Academic Librarian." *Library Trends* 64, no. 4 (2016).

Tong, Rosemary. *Feminine and Feminist Ethics.* Belmont, CA: Wadsworth Publishing Companing, 1993.

Ukeles, Miere Laderman. "Manifesto for Maintenance Art, 1969! Proposal for an Exhibition 'Care.'" http://www.feldmangallery.com/media/pdfs/Ukeles_MANIFESTO.pdf.

Van Slyck, Abigail A. *Free to All: Carnegie Libraries & American Culture, 1890-1920.* Chicago: University of Chicago Press, 1995.

On the Disparity Between What We Say and What We Do in Libraries

Baharak Yousefi

In July of 2014, a woman named Trish Kelly was running as a candidate for a seat on Vancouver's park board with Vision Vancouver, a center-left civic party in Vancouver, British Columbia. She had won the most votes in a nomination race on the party's slate and was, in many people's minds, a clear front-runner in the election. In her own words, "After 25 years of serving my community, I put my name forward as a Park Board nominee to move my life as a community activist fighting for social justice issues, to claiming a seat at the decision-making table."[1] Kelly is also a sex positive artist and in 2006, she had performed in a video where she was filmed walking down the street and talking about masturbation as part of a series by Way Out West TV, a LGBTQ online TV station. The piece is funny, provocative, honest, and it was never hidden by Kelly. A Vancouver blogger named Raymond Tomlin wrote a blog post about this *"potentially* explosive"[2] [emphasis in original] video and a short while later, Kelly stepped down. The official response from Vision Vancouver was that they did

---

1 Charlie Smith, "Trish Kelly Quits as Vision Vancouver Park Candidate to Halt Distractions Over Her Sex-positive Activism," *The Georgia Straight*, July 14, 2014. Accessed January 20, 2017, http://www.straight.com/news/688731/trish-kelly-quits-vision-vancouver-park-candidate-halt-distractions-over-her-sex-positive-activism.

2 Raymond Tomlin, "Decision 2014: Another Shiny Nail in the Vision Vancouver Coffin," *Vanramblings.com* (blog), July 14, 2014. Accessed January 30, 2017, http://www.vanramblings.com/decision-2014-another-nail-in-the-vision-vancouver-coffin.html.

not want to divert attention from the issues of the election and keeping Kelly on the ballot would have been too distracting for Vancouver residents. Kelly is a queer woman of Métis and Ukrainian descent, a demographic not typically found on the ballot in the City's municipal elections. Many Vancouverites were frustrated with Vision Vancouver and wanted to come together to discuss and debate the issues; they wanted to talk about democracy, diversity, and what it is like to be a woman and a woman of Indigenous descent in Canadian politics. One Vancouver resident, a supporter of Kelly, contacted the university library where I work to ask if we would be willing to host a panel discussion with Trish Kelly and other experts. After a few internal conversations, we concluded that our library was not the "best unit" to host an event of this nature. A few days later, the event took place at the university but without the support or involvement of the library.

I share this story here not because it is particularly unique or remarkable, but because it is illustrative of the disconnect between our professional values of democracy and social responsibility[3] and our decisions and actions. We routinely make decisions that oppose our declared values. We decline opportunities to host forums on democracy and citizen engagement. We choose library vendors that do not align with our stated goals and principles. We claim intellectual freedom as a core value, but silence professional dissent within our own ranks. And—disturbingly—we seem to get away with it with few or no repercussions. My main questions, and the reasons for this exploratory chapter, are what are the systems that help create and sustain the disparity between what we say and what we do in libraries? And can we disrupt these systems in ways that are both viable and generative?

It is useful, I believe, to consider the situation I describe in the example above and others like it not in terms of what is being declared, in value statements for example, but instead in terms of what is being done or not being done. What is the action or inaction? I find a compelling analog in Keller Easterling's critical spatial/political analysis, in particular in her work on what she calls "infrastructure space," where she probes the discrepancies between what is said and

---

3 American Library Association, "Core Values of Librarianship," Adopted June 29, 2004, http://www.ala.org/advocacy/intfreedom/statementspols/corevalues.

what is done.[4] Easterling's concept of infrastructure space goes beyond what she describes as "object forms" such as buildings, roads, policies, strategic plans, and value statements, to probe "active forms"—the undeclared rules and activities that form the disposition or propensity of a system, be it a city, an organization, or a free trade zone. According to Easterling, while we act in relation to object forms, our actions are also influenced by de facto forms of power that are often more consequential than our official positions. In libraries, our policies, strategic plans, and value statements are examples of our official positions; they are the object forms of our profession. Yet, there are forces that are more influential on our daily actions than what we document and declare. Easterling explains this dynamic: "It is not the pattern printed on the fabric but the way the fabric floats. It is not the shape of the game piece but the way the game piece plays. It is not the text but the constantly updating software that manages the text."[5]

Casting our eye away from the object forms of our profession is useful because it allows us to examine our character, which results from the interconnections and totality of our activities—our active form. It will allow us to examine the influential and yet undeclared information about the profession, which resides in our protocols, routines, and myriad other instances of active form that create the infrastructure space of librarianship. In the Trish Kelly example at the beginning of this chapter, the ALA "Core Values of Librarianship" statement[6] declaring our professional commitment to democracy and social responsibility is the object form, while our refusal to host this event is the expression of our active form. In *Extrastatecraft,* Easterling writes about infrastructure:

> The word "infrastructure" typically conjures associations with physical networks for transportation, communication, or utilities. Infrastructure is considered to be a hidden substrate—the binding medium or current between objects of positive consequence, shape, and law. Yet today, more than grids of pipes and wires… [t]he shared standards and ideas that control everything from technical objects to management styles also constitute an infrastructure. Far from

---

4 Keller Easterling, *Extrastatecraft: The Power of Infrastructure Space* (New York: Verso, 2014).

5 Ibid., 21.

6 American Library Association, "Core Values of Librarianship," Adopted June 29, 2004, http://www.ala.org/advocacy/intfreedom/statementspols/corevalues

hidden, infrastructure is now the overt point of contact and access between us all—the rules governing the space of everyday life.[7]

She further illustrates the significance of this space: "Contemporary infrastructure space is the secret weapon of the most powerful people in the world precisely because it orchestrates activities that can remain unstated but are nevertheless consequential."[8]

There are of course a myriad of historical, socio-political, cultural, and institutional forces—big and small—at play in every library which contribute to forming its organizational character. But for the purposes of this discussion, I am keen to consider the infrastructure. Since the beginning of my work as a practitioner in Canadian libraries almost a decade ago, I have been interested in the details of how the culture and disposition of the profession is set, communicated, sometimes obscured, and policed in our everyday practice. More recently, after I became a middle manager with a significant amount of decision-making power, this interest became more pronounced as I struggled to reconcile the belief that our decisions are made in accordance with our values, policies, and resources with the reality that there are significant disparities between what we say and what we do. For example, at the 2015 Association of College and Research Libraries Conference in Portland, Oregon, a ballroom full of librarians sat listening to Lawrence Lessig talk about the tragic death of American computer programmer, activist, and open access advocate Aaron Swartz at a conference sponsored by library vendors who actively oppose Lessig's call for equality and equal access to knowledge.[9] There is something disconcerting about our ability to dissociate ourselves personally from our collective actions and responsibilities. It is as though my inaction and my lack of protest as an individual librarian is not part-and-parcel of the greater cultural and professional whole. Of course, this is a familiar group dynamic, but what makes our situation particularly interesting is that libraries and librarians claim to be organized around progressive ideals both on institutional and individual levels. Perhaps this understanding of ourselves as "being on the right side,"

---

7 Easterling, *Extrastatecraft*, 11.

8 Ibid., 15.

9 Lawrence Lessig, "Keynote," *ACRL 2015 Conference*, Accessed Feb 2, 2017, http://acrl. learningtimesevents.org/keynote-lessig/.

institutionally and professionally, allows some of us to dismiss the need or urgency for personal action. But it is important to probe and problematize our progressive professional rhetoric by looking at what we actually do. Easterling writes that "many disciplines are questioning their own presumptions and searching for alternative ways to adjust the global political landscape. Infrastructure space is a good test bed for these experiments—a complex matrix harbouring all kinds of social habits, cultural values, economies, and technologies. A web of active forms contributes to the disposition of infrastructure space—its immanent capacity, propensity, or political bearing."[10] This idea of an unseen and yet influential infrastructure space is reminiscent of Edgar Schein's model of organizational culture, where "basic underlying assumptions" or deeply embedded "beliefs, perceptions, thoughts, and feelings" which constitute the essence of an organization's culture, are a significant source of values and actions. In Schein's model, however, these assumptions often remain unconscious.[11] Easterling's notion of infrastructure space is different in its intentionality; it functions in active form without the threat of scrutiny typically reserved for object forms. For example, "diversity and inclusion" are mentioned explicitly as part of many library strategic plans and values statements across North America and yet the appetite and willingness to engender any significant cultural shift is not present in most of our institutions. As Chanda Prescod-Weinstein argues, "If you're serious about diversity, then you have to be serious about ending discrimination, and if you are serious about ending discrimination, then you have to be serious about letting go of your unearned power."[12] In libraries, as with all institutions, there are unconscious factors which inform our organizational cultures, but the decision to maintain the status quo, to preserve current power structures, and by extension to remain exclusionary, is intentional.

---

10 Easterling, *Extrastatecraft*, 239.

11 Edgar Schein, *Organizational Culture and Leadership* (San Francisco: Jossey-Bass Publishers, 1992), 17.

12 Chanda Prescod-Weinstein, "How to Make a Real Commitment to Diversity: A Guide for Faculty/Managers Especially," *Medium*, Aug 17, 2016. Accessed January 30, 2017, https://medium.com/@chanda/how-to-make-a-real-commitment-to-diversity-30ddb2cc4cc3#.2nkehrxmd.

In libraries, these disparities are increasingly less visible in our structures. We are, for example, diligent about using diversity statements in our job advertisements. They are, however, present in our infrastructures. For example, we continue to look for "fit" when hiring new librarians, which tends to mean more of the same: same backgrounds, same perspectives, same worldviews. While the concept of "neutrality" was and is still sometimes being used to maintain and perpetuate the status quo, the tactics have been changing. In my experience, we often relied on the language of neutrality to explain and justify our decisions. In the Trish Kelly incident, for example, we were keen to maintain neutrality and hosting her at our library would have signalled a non-neutral, political stance. This pursuit of neutrality in libraries has, in the past, provided an effective strategy to silence dissent and to secure consent from marginalized groups. At times, the appeals to remain neutral and impartial are explicit still, but there have been convincing arguments made against them in LIS literature[13] and so they have shifted shape. Now, they are most effective in restricting behaviors and decisions to acceptable levels of deviation from the norm in our seemingly benign responses and justifications (e.g. "the library is not the 'best unit' to support an event of this nature") or as Easterling puts it, in "the bits of code" that run this particular profession's "operating system."[14] And if the norm in North American librarianship is forged by decades of racism, sexism, white privilege, colonization, and institutional oppression,[15] then preserving the norm is an act of injustice.[16] Further, this infrastructure space of language, style, and practice evolves to respond to new conditions or behaviors. A few years ago, after arguing—not dispassionately—

---

13 Alison Lewis, ed., *Questioning Library Neutrality: Essays from Progressive Librarian* (Duluth: Library Juice Press, 2008);and Chris Bourg, "Never Neutral: Libraries, Technology, and Inclusion," *Feral Librarian* (blog), January 28, 2015. Accessed January 30, 2017. https://chrisbourg.wordpress.com/2015/01/28/never-neutral-libraries-technology-and-inclusion/.

14 Easterling, *Extrastatecraft*, 92.

15 nina de jesus, "Locating the Library in Institutional Oppression," *In the Library with a Lead Pipe*, September 24, 2014. Accessed January 30, 2017.

16 Nicole Pagowsky and Niamh Wallace, "Black Lives Matter! Shedding Library Neutrality Rhetoric for Social Justice," *College and Research Libraries News*. 76, 4(2015): 196-214, accessed January 30, 2017, http://crln.acrl.org/content/76/4/196.full.pdf.

against a particular policy decision, I was told by a colleague that the choice we were making was "not religious." This language caught me off guard. What I believe my colleague was saying is that we have to stay detached from the moral and ethical considerations of our decision; we have to stay "neutral." But it was said in this new way that was meant to unsettle, and to halt further objections and discussions. The language may be different but the results remain the same. The results are equally consequential. As Easterling argues "the things that make infrastructure space powerful are its multipliers, its irrational fictions, or its undeclared but consequential activities. They are also perhaps the very things that make it immune to righteous declaration or prescription. The rational, resolute, and righteous, while cornerstones of dissent, are sometimes less consequential than the discrepant, fictional, or sly."[17]

So what do we do? How do we interact with these practices in ways that increase the capacity and longevity of those who wish to unsettle and disrupt this infrastructure space? Activism and direct resistance play a significant role in this work, but what else? Remember, the rational and the righteous are less effective in this arena precisely because the crucial information about the profession cannot always be found in our vision, mission, and values statements or our strategic plans. It can, however, be inferred from our dispositions, our propensities, and the subtleties with which a particular agenda is pushed through while a different goal or intention is espoused. It is difficult to fight with indignation what is not there. Easterling advocates for an "expanded activist repertoire"[18] in infrastructure space. While there are times to oppose injustice directly and openly, there are also times to resist in tacit ways that exploit the differences between our professional declarations and our actions. Easterling elaborates on context: "There are times to stand up, name an opponent, or assume a binary stance of resistance against authoritarian power, but supplementing these forms of dissent are activist stances that are both harder to target and less interested in being right."[19] In the library profession, if those with power do something different than what they are saying, then are there ways to use what is being said in the service of disruption alongside of active, open resistance? Released

---

17 Easterling, *Extrastatecraft*, 23.

18 Ibid., 213.

19 Ibid., 213.

from "the tense grip of binary resistance,"[20] can we wreak havoc in infrastructure space? Among Easterling's expanded activist repertoire, I have chosen four techniques to explore in the context of libraries: gossip, doubling, hacking[21], and exaggerated compliance.[22]

Whether we call it storytelling, rumor, or telling tales, gossip is an old strategy and can be a profoundly political act. Talking has always been dangerous for those in power. Easterling sees it as a common tool for decentering power and creating alternative narratives.[23] I further see it as a significant tool of information sharing with and among marginalized individuals and groups—a possible way to subvert established norms, procedures, and assumptions. And it is not necessarily for our own benefit that we tell tales; we can help others by talking as well. By telling our stories, we may help reduce the epistemic doubt of others. For example, in a profession where approximately nine out of ten credentialed librarians are white,[24] "gossip" can play an essential role for minority librarians. I have lost count of the number of times I have left a conversation or interaction and wondered, "Did he say what I think he said? Did others hear him? Was it all in my head?" If, instead of going our separate ways quietly and "professionally," we took the time as colleagues to speak informally about what we saw, heard, or what others have seen or heard, these observations and histories would begin to give shape to patterns—patterns that can help us gain confidence in what we see, hear, and experience. Saba Fatima writes, "As women of colour, we are greatly underrepresented in academia. This adversely impacts our ability to speak about our experiences with an expectation of understanding such encounters by our allies. And when one is constantly given alternate banal explanations for their overly sensitive perceptions, one loses the epistemic ground they stand on. [We] cease

---

20 Ibid., 215.

21 Easterling uses the phrase "hacker/entrepreneur" to describe this particular tactic, but I have made the decision to use hacker and hacking alone as I find it more evocative and relevant to the library context.

22 Easterling, *Extrastatecraft*, 213.

23 Ibid., 214.

24 American Library Association, "Diversity Counts," Updated 2012, http://www.ala.org/offices/diversity/diversitycounts/divcounts.

to give credibility to [our] own perceptions."[25] Talking about your daily experiences in the workplace helps others keep a tighter grasp on their own reality. Malinda Smith describes stories as forms of communication that weave together individual minority experiences into meaningful, situated episodes.[26] Our discretion is being counted on to maintain the status quo. By keeping the marginalized in a state of uncertainty and self-doubt, the powerful gain time to repeat, reinforce, and reproduce—to consolidate their power. Imagine a librarian of color coming out of a meeting and gossiping with her colleague about what they both heard. Imagine her being told that she is not being too sensitive or too defensive and that she did, in fact, hear what she thinks she heard. Witnessing and acknowledgement can be powerful tools in disrupting the status quo. It is time to start talking.

A second tactic of resistance in infrastructure space is doubling, where Easterling describes the double as "not only as a source of competition but also an opportunity for confusion and disguise. The double… can sometimes fool the world or launder an identity. A double can simply hijack the place of power of its counterpart to increase its territory in the world."[27] The tactic of working within existing structures, even if you are ultimately opposed to them, in order to bring about change, is a familiar strategy. April Hathcock has written about the idea of taking on an identity to take power.[28] Hathcock has referred to this as "playing at whiteness," which in the context of librarians of color in libraries, she defines to mean playing the game, getting in, and then doing what we want and making room for others to do the same. "It is important that those of us in LIS with privilege—be it the privilege of actual whiteness or the privilege of skill in playing whiteness—serve as effective allies to those who do not. We need to make space for our

---

25 Saba Fatima, "Am I Being Paranoid? Being a Woman of Color in Academia." *SIUE Women's Studies Program Blog.* April 20, 2015. Accessed January 30, 2017, https://siuewmst.wordpress.com/2015/04/20/am-i-being-paranoid-being-a-woman-of-color-in-academia/.

26 Malinda Smith, "Gender, Whiteness and the 'Other Others' in the Academy,"in *States of Race: Critical Race Feminism for the 21st Century,* ed. S. Razack, M. Smith, and Thobani, S. (Toronto: Between the Lines Press, 2010) 37-58.

27 Easterling, *Extrastatecraft,* 222.

28 April Hathcock, "White Librarianship in Blackface: Diversity Initiatives in LIS," *In the Library with a Lead Pipe,* October 7, 2015. Accessed January 30, 2017, http://www.inthelibrarywiththeleadpipe.org/2015/lis-diversity/.

diverse colleagues to thrive within the profession. In short, we need to dismantle whiteness from within LIS," Hathcock argues."[29] I find the immediacy and impact of this tactic to be particularly enticing. Serving as an ally can take many forms, both big and small, and the impact of one individual who helps clear the path for another cannot be overstated. As doubles, we would not need to necessarily engage on a policy level to disrupt or interfere with the status quo, even if systemic change remains our overarching goal.

Another strategy, which Sara Ahmed refers to as "inhabiting whiteness,"[30] is related but different from the deliberate doubling proposed by Easterling and described by Hathcock above. In this case, people of color surrounded by institutional whiteness in academe (and in libraries), inhabit whiteness as a survival strategy. Over time, we train ourselves to not see it: "I had become so used to this whiteness that I had stopped noticing it."[31] While the strategy may allow us to enter and stay working in the profession, Ahmed also warns of the emotional and psychic toll it can take—a toll that is hard to fully appreciate until we have the opportunity to unburden ourselves: "When you inhabit a sea of brownness as a person of colour you might realise the effort of your previous inhabitance, as the effort of not noticing what is around you. It is like how you can feel the 'weight' of tiredness most acutely as the tiredness leaves you. To become conscious of how things leave you is to become conscious of those things. We might become even more aware of whiteness as wearing, when we leave the spaces of whiteness."[32] Walking home after attending an event at Indian Summer Festival,[33] I found myself weeping unexpectedly. It took just a couple of minutes to recognize the relief and catharsis of having just left a theater full of brown people. "It can be surprising and energizing not to feel so singular."[34] The reasons why underrepresented individuals leave librarianship at a higher

---

29 Ibid.

30 Sara Ahmed, *On Being Included: Racism and Diversity in Institutional Life* (Durham: Duke University Press, 2012), 35.

31 Ibid., 35.

32 Ibid., 36.

33 An annual multi-arts festival in Vancouver, Canada with an emphasis on artists and performers from South Asia.

34 Ahmed, *On Being Included*, 36.

rate than others is an open research question,[35] but it is not difficult to imagine that the labor that is required to inhabit and double—even when it is done in service and as strategy—does take a toll. In the library world, the hacker is a close ally of the double. While she may not have to explicitly or intentionally assume an identity to infiltrate the space of power, the hacker is committed to the long game of progressive change. Writes Easterling: "[The hacker] does not value purity but rather relies on multiple cycles of innovation, updating platforms, and tracking changeable desires that supersede, refresh, or reverse the products and plans they introduce into the world."[36] Her work, which can span the range of the activist repertoire, persists as smaller corrective measures. She is not daunted by nor is she seeking "a transcendent and singular moment of change—a comprehensive reform or a soulful masterpiece."[37] For example, the librarian who co-opts and subverts existing structures such as library display spaces to showcase progressive publications or the librarian who works to eliminate library fines by implementing smaller measures such as reminder emails, grace periods, or low fine cards for patrons with no fixed address—both fit the profile of the hacker. With the long-term goal of progressive change or equitable access in mind, these hackers make use of smaller opportunities to initiate shifts and make modifications. I admire the tenacity of the hacker and applaud her commitment to moving the dial in a profession which not only resists, but also works to undermine her efforts. I am grateful for her steadfastness and ingenuity, and acknowledge her focused change-making in a space that she sees anew for its potential for political action.

The last tactic in Easterling's expanded activist repertoire that I will discuss in the LIS context is exaggerated compliance. As a middle manager I have found that when it comes to openness and transparency, two professional values that we tend to declare widely and practice scarcely, exaggerated compliance can be a powerful tool. I have made a practice of investigating what information I am actually supposed to keep confidential (surprisingly few things are

---

35 Jennifer Vinopal, "The Quest for Diversity in Library Staffing: From Awareness to Action," *In the Library with a Lead Pipe*, January 13, 2016. Accessed January 30, 2017, http://www.inthelibrarywiththeleadpipe.org/2016/quest-for-diversity/.

36 Easterling, *Extrastatecraft*, 232.

37 Ibid., 231.

in that category in some academic libraries) and what information I can share with others. I have made a conscious decision to discuss everything that I am technically allowed to talk about with my staff and colleagues. Similar to the disruptive processes that I discussed in relation to the tactic of "gossip," I find that discretion and to some level arrogance—more so than mandated confidentiality—is at play when institutions who declare their commitment to transparency manage to keep their workers in the dark and out of decision making loops. Our discretion can be relied upon to keep non-confidential information confidential and further promote an unequal access to information by reinforcing the patronizing and false assumption that people would simply not be interested. I tend to not worry too much about whether or not people are actually interested in the information I am sharing, but rather I know that in being transparent I can learn from those in positions without easy access to this information. I know that by being a conduit for information, by becoming part of the infrastructure in this exaggerated way, I reduce my own chances of one day claiming one thing and doing another, of becoming propelled toward injustice. Ahmed writes about the importance of careful hesitation: "There is no guarantee that in struggling for justice we ourselves will be just. We have to hesitate, to temper the strength of our tendencies with doubt; to waver when we are sure, or even because we are sure. A feminist movement that proceeds with too much confidence has cost us too much already. We falter with feminist conviction. As we must."[38] I see an exaggerated commitment to transparency as fostering a system of checks and balances for me both personally and professionally.

I believe that accountability is a cornerstone of feminist leadership, but it is difficult to be held accountable if one does not actively provide an opportunity for others to evaluate us and hold us to account. As feminists and as feminists in leadership positions, we make mistakes. All we can hope for is that we are deserving of a community of colleagues who are willing to call us in. Ngọc Loan Trần defines calling in as the "practice of pulling folks back in who have strayed from us. It means extending to ourselves the reality that we will and do fuck up, we stray and there will always be a chance for us to return. Calling in as a practice of loving each other enough to allow each other to make mistakes; a practice of loving ourselves enough to know that what we're

---

38 Sara Ahmed, "Losing Confidence," *feministkilljoys* (blog). March 1, 2016. Accessed January 30, 2017, https://feministkilljoys.com/2016/03/01/losing-confidence/.

trying to do here is a radical unlearning of everything we have been configured to believe is normal."[39] In the past two decades of working in supervisory and leadership roles in and out of libraries, I have time and time again been called in by friends and colleagues who have listened to my uninformed opinions and put up with my inexperience. And they have stuck around as I struggled and learned. They have done this because they are generous and kind, and my greatest hope going forward is that they are willing to do it over and over again. The very least I can do in response to these acts of grace and generosity is to practice uncompromising openness and transparency.

One of the early catalysts for this exploratory chapter was the realization that in libraries the presence of one or two librarians of color is the full extent of our commitment to "diversity and inclusion." Our presence is not, as I had assumed for years, a harbinger. It is not a signal that we are all here to do the work of unlearning and undoing that is necessary for substantive, structural change. The change, it seems to me, is considered complete on our arrival. In my experience, libraries are open to diverse populations as long as that diversity does not extend to how we behave, speak, or think. While the content of this chapter is not wholly or necessarily related to the lack of anti-racist and anti-colonial work in our profession, our declarations about the importance of diversity and inclusion while actively protecting the status quo and fostering sameness, has been a significant site of struggle for me personally. In the larger infrastructure space of this profession, it is necessary to scrutinize our actions and inactions in light of our declared values and intentions on multiple critical fronts, and I believe that many of us have and continue to do so. It is my hope that Easterling's concept of infrastructure space, as applied to everything from management style to daily practice, can help us to see our actions, our propensities, and our trajectories as deliberate, but also entities that can be resisted and reshaped by familiar as well as unconventional tactics—an expanded activist repertoire. It is my hope that we can understand and utilize these tactics not only as supplements to open dissent, but also as mechanisms that will allow us to organize and develop coalitions for future resistance.

---

39 Ngọc Loan Trần, "Calling IN: A Less Disposable Way of Holding Each Other Accountable," *Black Girl Dangerous* (blog), December 18, 2013. Accessed July 15, 2015, http://www.blackgirldangerous.org/2013/12/calling-less-disposable-way-holding-accountable.

References

Ahmed, Sara. *On Being Included: Racism and Diversity in Institutional Life*. Durham: Duke University Press, 2012.

American Library Association. "Core Values of Librarianship." Adopted June 29, 2004. http://www.ala.org/advocacy/intfreedom/ statementspols/corevalues. American Library Association. "Diversity Counts," Updated 2012. http://www.ala.org/offices/ diversity/diversitycounts/divcounts.

Bourg, Chris. "Never Neutral: Libraries, Technology, and Inclusion." *Feral Librarian*, January 28, 2015. Accessed January 30, 2017. https://chrisbourg.wordpress.com/2015/01/28/never-neutral-libraries-technology-and-inclusion/.

de jesus, nina. "Locating the Library in Institutional Oppression." *In the Library with a Lead Pipe*, September 24, 2014. Accessed January 30, 2017. http://www.inthelibrarywiththeleadpipe. org/2014/locating-the-library-in-institutional-oppression.

Easterling, Keller. *Extrastatecraft: The Power of Infrastructure Space*. New York: Verso, 2014.

Fatima, Saba. "Am I Being Paranoid? Being a Woman of Color in Academia." *SIUE Women's Studies Program Blog*, April 20, 2015. Accessed January 30, 2017. https://siuewmst.wordpress. com/2015/04/20/am-i-being-paranoid-being-a-woman-of-color-in-academia/.

Hathcock, April. "White Librarianship in Blackface: Diversity Initiatives in LIS." *In the Library with a Lead Pipe*, October 7, 2015. Accessed January 30, 2017. http://www. inthelibrarywiththeleadpipe.org/2015/lis-diversity/.

Lessig, Lawrence. "Keynote," *ACRL 2015 Conference* video, Accessed Feb 2, 2017. http://acrl.learningtimesevents.org/keynote-lessig/.

Lewis, Alison, ed. *Questioning Library Neutrality: Essays from Progressive Librarian*. Duluth: Library Juice Press, 2008

Pagowsky, Nicole and Niamh Wallace, "Black Lives Matter! Shedding Library Neutrality Rhetoric for Social Justice." *College and*

Research Libraries News, 76, 4, (2015): 196-214, accessed January 30, 2017. http://crln.acrl.org/content/76/4/196.full.pdf.

Prescod-Weinstein, Chanda. "How to Make a Real Commitment to Diversity: A Guide for Faculty/Managers Especially. *Medium*, Aug 17, 2016. Accessed January 30, 2017. https://medium.com/@chanda/how-to-make-a-real-commitment-to-diversity-30ddb2cc4cc3#.2nkehrxmd.

Schein, Edgar. *Organizational Culture and Leadership*. San Francisco: Jossey-Bass Publishers, 1992.

Smith, Charlie. "Trish Kelly Quits as Vision Vancouver Park Candidate to Halt Distractions Over Her Sex-positive Activism." *The Georgia Straight*, July 14, 2014. Accessed January 20, 2017. http://www.straight.com/news/688731/trish-kelly-quits-vision-vancouver-park-candidate-halt-distractions-over-her-sex-positive-activism.

Smith, Malinda. "Gender, Whiteness and the 'Other Others' in the Academy." In *States of Race: Critical Race Feminism for the 21st Century*, edited by S. Razack, M. Smith, and S. Thobani, 37-58. Toronto: Between the Lines Press, 2010.

Tomlin, Raymond. "Decision 2014: Another Shiny Nail in the Vision Vancouver Coffin." *Vanramblings.com* (blog), July 14, 2014. Accessed January 30, 2017. http://www.vanramblings.com/decision-2014-another-nail-in-the-vision-vancouver-coffin.html.

Trần, Ngọc Loan. "Calling IN: A Less Disposable Way of Holding Each Other Accountable." *Black Girl Dangerous*, December 18, 2013. Accessed July 15, 2015. http://www.blackgirldangerous.org/2013/12/calling-less-disposable-way-holding-accountable.

Vinopal, Jennifer. "The Quest for Diversity in Library Staffing: From Awareness to Action." *In the Library with a Lead Pipe*, January 13, 2016. Accessed January 30, 2017. http://www.inthelibrarywiththeleadpipe.org/2016/quest-for-diversity/.

How We Speak, How We Think, What We Do: Leading Intersectional Feminist Conversations in Libraries

Rachel Fleming and Kelly McBride

Introduction

As the authors of this chapter contemplated feminist leadership in libraries, the issues that rose to the top related most to the intersectionality of the authors. We observed that discussions about diversity and inclusion within our library are often limited and opportunistic. It is perplexing that important conversations about diversity are not happening and at the same time, it seems that the responsibility for starting, leading, and sustaining these conversations rests not with majority but with the minority. As librarians, we talk about many parts of our lives and our practice, but there is often a brick wall when issues related to diversity and inclusion come up. So the authors set out to explore for ourselves, as academic librarians, how we speak, how we think, and what we do in relation to this topic.

This chapter is an exploration that required the authors to step outside our normal roles and comfort zones to share our thoughts and experiences. Researching and writing this chapter represents our first foray into formal leadership on diversity as well as our first public discussion about diversity in the profession. After situating ourselves in our intersectional identities, and acknowledging the limitations of our perceptions, we will describe the current state of conversations about diversity and inclusion in libraries and the library profession as we see it. We will explore strategies for building awareness and being intentional about what we do and don't do within the library profession related to diversity and inclusion; discuss the importance of contextualizing conversations about diversity, inclusion, and oppression in the workplace; examine issues such as microaggressions and fragility; address how we deal with our own hang ups; discuss the vital importance of self-care and support; and identify suggestions for leading the way forward.

The authors make no claim of expertise—our areas of specialization are not diversity, inclusion, implicit bias, anti-racism, or any other fields closely related to anti-oppression work. Our knowledge is based in our own experiences in and out of the workplace and in the collective knowledge of the marginalized groups to which we belong. We want to share observations from our particular locations in discussions about these specific topics. Indeed, we acknowledge our complicity in the problem through our own failure to act. We hope that these observations and analysis are a valuable place to begin leading organizations forward into deeper and more meaningful conversations.

BACKGROUNDS AND LIMITATIONS OF PERCEPTION

From our perspectives, the most impactful feminist actions in libraries would address not only issues of sexism, but also issues of race, homophobia, and other oppressions. We base this chapter on both research and the experiences of the authors, personal and professional, including discussions with our colleagues and friends. Our views are fundamentally shaped by our identities, which exist at a myriad of intersections. Our professional experiences as academic librarians in small to medium sized colleges and regional universities frame our perception. Rachel Fleming is young, Jewish, queer, genderqueer, single, and white. Kelly McBride is middle-aged, Christian, black, heterosexual, female, and married (part of an interracial couple). However, these labels fail to reveal our multifaceted identities and experiences. The manner in which conversations about underrepresented groups, systemic oppressions, and implicit biases occur (or more often don't occur) in our organizations distinguished itself as an area of mutual concern and experience.

Conversations We Are Not Having

In the experience of the authors, and in conversations with others in the profession, we find that organization-wide conversations seem almost scripted to meet a perceived need to speak to diversity as defined by our libraries and professional organizations. The most common conversations may be in the context of the hiring process, diversity training, and diversity programming. Notwithstanding the benefits, each of these initiatives are also controlled, contained, and vetted. This type of programming focuses on specific, limited action. While each program may increase awareness, the impact of intersectional conversations, rather than diversity programming, would be greater. As Brook et al. point out, "the ways in which these discussions have taken place are problematic...once again affirming that Whiteness is the neutral, normal way of being in libraries."[1] Many individuals within an organization continually engage in much deeper intersectional conversations about diversity and inclusion. Members of underrepresented groups tend to gather and discuss issues of systemic oppression and implicit bias within the professional setting. These conversations also serve as a release valve for members of underrepresented groups where mutual support is shared. Deeper conversations have always occurred, but they do not seem to spread throughout the organization.

Compared to diversity programming, intersectional conversations offer an opportunity for deeper engagement with issues, creating affective change. Intersectional conversations are conversations that engage in issues of diversity and inclusion with respect and deference to the range of experiences of those involved in the conversations. Intersectional conversations require a level of vulnerability and willingness to engage with no promise of outcomes. These conversations require a greater commitment than traditional diversity programming by both individuals and organizations. Some middle ground between superficial discussions that occur sporadically throughout the organization and meaningful conversations that occur in select and selective groups is a reasonable and attainable goal in many organizations.

---

1 Freeda Brook, Dave Ellenwood, and Althea Eannance Lazzaro, "In Pursuit of Antiracist Social Justice: Denaturalizing Whiteness in the Academic Library," *Library Trends* 64(2): 247.

The organizational benefits of diversity are well documented. The American Library Association names diversity as "a fundamental value" of the library profession.[2] Diversity is also included as one of the Key Action Areas in the American Library Association (ALA) Strategic Plan:

> Libraries play a crucial role in empowering diverse populations for full participation in a Democratic society. In the library workforce, programs of recruitment, training, development, advancement and promotion are needed in order to increase and retain diverse library personnel who are reflective of the society we serve. Within the Association and in the services and operations of libraries, efforts to include diversity in programs, activities, services, professional literature, products and continuing education must be ongoing and encouraged.[3]

However, statistics from the ALA Demographic Studies indicate that the library profession remains overwhelming white. ALA's 2012 Diversity Counts study show that in 2000, 88.9% of credentialed librarians were white, and in 2009-2010, 87.9%.[4] A 2014 demographic study of ALA members reported 87.1% of respondents as white.[5] National associations have a number of initiatives in place designed to increase diversity among professional ranks. Two initiatives are Spectrum, a scholarship program designed to create an ethnically diverse workforce, research grants, and the Committee on Diversity, an ALA group charged with identifying national diversity issues and trends.[6] Although these efforts provide support to members of

2 American Library Association, "Diversity, Equity, and Inclusion." Accessed June 13, 2016. http://www.ala.org/advocacy/diversity.

3 American Library Association, "American Library Association Strategic Plan." Accessed August 27, 2016. http://www.ala.org/aboutala/sites/ala.org.aboutala/files/content/governance/StrategicPlan/Strategic%20Directions%20June%2028%202015.pdf).

4 American Library Association, "Diversity Counts 2012 Tables." Accessed August 27, 2016. http://www.ala.org/offices/sites/ala.org.offices/files/content/diversity/diversitycounts/diversitycountstables2012.pdf.

5 American Library Association, "ALA Demographics Studies." Accessed August 27, 2016. ww.ala.org/research/sites/ala.org.research/files/content/initiatives/membershipsurveys/September2014ALADemographics.pdf.

6 American Library Association, "Recruiting for Diversity." Accessed August 27, 2016. http://www.ala.org/advocacy/diversity/workforcedevelopment/recruitmentfordiversity.

underrepresented groups entering the library profession, there is still much work to be done.

While diversity is a strongly stated value in the profession, we have not seen the kind of widespread change that would be expected. Professional organizations support the development of diverse professionals, reflecting a tendency to focus on increasing the numbers of professionals from marginalized groups, rather than on cultural shifts toward inclusion of diverse viewpoints to serve diverse needs. Diversity itself, "the condition or quality of being diverse, different, or varied"[7] does not require change in dominant cultures. Change is required by inclusiveness, the "practice or policy of not excluding any person, on the grounds of race, gender, religion, age, or disability."[8] Inclusive organizations are better positioned to serve diverse patrons and offer opportunities to diverse librarians. Organizational inclusivity cannot be achieved by simply increasing the number of professionals from underrepresented groups. A focus on numbers alone can result in an increase in diversity which might not translate into valuing, appreciating, or accepting people from diverse backgrounds and experiences. Jennifer Vinopal points out that societal trends suggest that while the majority of Americans profess support of diversity, their actions do not show that support in workplaces. Vinopal raises the question "how much diversity is enough to make staff in the dominant culture, race, ethnicity, sexual identity, etc. feel like the workplace has achieved an acceptable amount of but not too much diversity?"[9] As a result of unclear and unmeasurable organizational goals related to diversity, search committees, diversity training, and diversity programs can be a performance of diversity without any actual diversity or inclusivity outcomes. While attendance at each event can be counted, this may not translate into a broader examination of what specific effort was made, toward what goal, and to what affect. Without a mandate to do so, thoughtful assessment and improvement of existing initiatives will not occur. Organization-wide intersectional conversations provide a foundation to introduce and encourage

---

7 OED Online, September 2016, s.v. "diversity."

8 OED Online, September 2016, s.v. "inclusiveness."

9 Jennifer Vinopal, "The Quest or Diversity in Library Staffing: From Awareness o Action." *In the Library with The Lead Pipe*, January 13, 2016. http://www.inthelibrarywiththeleadpipe.org/2016/quest-for-diversity/.

inclusivity in a holistic way. The conversations and the programming are connected in a way that can be part of a broader shift toward inclusive organizational culture.[10]

Building Awareness & Intentionality

The library profession has stated goals related to diversity from both professional associations and many individual libraries.[11] Creating awareness and intentionality about conversations is an important first step toward an inclusive culture. When it comes to diversity initiatives within the profession, it is imperative that librarians learn from each other and understand how the goals of various initiatives can support efforts within their own libraries. The language of strategic plans does not always transfer into actionable items. In order to move toward an inclusive culture, goals need to be understood and written with clear, attainable outcomes situated in the context of diversity as a core value and strategic direction. Librarians often frame diversity itself as an organizational goal to be met. This framing allows libraries to meet the goal of having diversity within the organization without becoming an inclusive organization. We believe the goal of diversity is to foster a culture of inclusion that facilitates organizational change, and that an inclusive culture will in turn support diversity. According to business researcher Katherine Phillips, diversity in an organization "encourages the search for novel information and perspectives, leading to better decision making and problem solving."[12] In the library field, Jennifer Vinopal states, "Unless we are clear about what we are trying to accomplish and why and unless we're willing to name and examine

---

10 Angela Galvan, "Soliciting Performance, Hiding Bias: Whiteness and Librarianship," *In The Library With The Lead Pipe*, June 3, 2015, http://www.inthelibrarywiththeleadpipe.org/2015/soliciting-performance-hiding-bias-whiteness-and-librarianship/.

11 American Library Association, "American Library Association Strategic Directions." Accessed August 27, 2016, http://www.ala.org/aboutala/sites/ala.org.aboutala/files/content/governance/StrategicPlan/Strategic%20Directions%20June%2028%202015.pdf.

12 Katherine W. Phillips, "How Diversity Makes Us Smarter: Being Around People Who Are Different From Us Makes Us More Creative, More Diligent And Harder-Working," *Scientific American*, October 1, 2014, accessed November 22, 2016, http://www.scientificamerican.com/article/how-diversity-makes-us-smarter/.

the underlying factors that thwart the changes we hope to see, we will ultimately fail."[13]

It is possible to raise intersectional concerns when addressing almost any library-related issue. To create an environment where it is more likely that intersectional concerns can be raised, it is important to first accept that bias is part of the human condition. Halvorson and Rock state that "human biases occur outside the conscious awareness, and thus people are literally unaware of them as they occur."[14] Halvorson and Rock also provide context on types of biases that are particularly endemic in organizational culture. In-group Bias (a type of similarity bias) is defined as "perceiving people who are similar to you (in ethnicity, religion, socioeconomic status, profession, etc.) more positively."[15] Awareness of in-group bias is essential because dominant cultures can self-perpetuate through this type of bias. Creating space where in-group bias is intentionally addressed allows us to more fully see the range of possibilities for our organizations. By continually questioning bias, libraries can move toward an inclusive culture.

Contextualizing the Conversations

In order to begin transformative conversations about diversity and inclusion in the workplace, librarians must address the experience of systemic oppression within their specific organizational cultures. Hearing and valuing the experiences of colleagues from underrepresented groups is the first step and a difficult one. Deflective responses like "that doesn't happen here" and "I've never seen that type of behavior" are second nature for many of us. Emotional, individual responses to oppression can serve to obscure the systemic nature of oppression. Feelings are real and have impacts, but it is also important to step back and analyze the many factors contributing to oppression which allows us to see the broader picture.

---

13 Vinopal, "The Quest for Diversity in Library Staffing."

14 Heidi Grant Halvorson and David Rock, "Beyond Bias: Neuroscience Research Shows How New Organizational Practices Can Shift Ingrained Thinking," *strategy + business*, July 13, 2015, Accessed November 22, 2016, http://www.strategy-business.com/article/00345.

15 Ibid.

Defining systemic oppression provides a framework around which organizations can begin to have productive conversations about diversity and inclusion. One useful set of definitions of systemic oppression has been published by Race Forward, an organization focused on building awareness of racial justice.[16] As part of their report "Moving the Race Conversation Forward," Race Forward defines four levels of bias, moving from individual to systemic.[17] While their work is focused on race, the frame is useful in understanding many oppressions. Race Forward's definition of individual oppression includes internalized and interpersonal bias. In media coverage and popular discourse, individual oppression is often the focus, which serves to "stifle the general public's understanding of systemic racism."[18] Systemic oppression includes systems of policies and practices in organizations that produce inequitable outcomes—institutional oppression—as well as the cumulative effect of historical and cultural factors that produce structural oppression.[19] A systems analysis places individual occurrences within a context of historical and cultural underpinnings. Adding the depth of context to discussions about diversity through a systems analysis "reveals root causes and contributing factors, and surfaces possible corresponding solutions."[20]

None of us want to believe that we are a part of an oppressive culture or that our actions further oppression. Perpetuating structures of oppression, intentionally or unintentionally, is common and must be confronted even among members of marginalized groups. Approaching conversations with attention to depth and context may address some of the stumbling blocks. A systems analysis allows individuals to identify which structures work for and against them as well as how these systemic intersections impact their daily life.

---

16 Race Forward / The Center for Racial Justice Innovation, "About Race Forward," accessed October 10, 2016, https://www.raceforward.org/about.

17 Race Forward / The Center for Racial Justice Innovation, "Moving The Race Conversation Forward: How The Media Covers Racism, And Other Barriers To Productive Racial Discourse: Part 1," accessed August 27, 2016, https://www.raceforward.org/research/reports/moving-race-conversation-forward.

18 Ibid., 3.

19 Ibid., 3.

20 Ibid., 3.

Further, understanding the complex structures of oppression allow libraries and librarians to identify how systemic oppression and exclusion is enacted by library organizations.

The work of libraries can be reduced to a series of tasks, reducing the focus on the mission and goals of libraries, including diversity and inclusion. Library workers can become disconnected from the impact that their work has in the broader community and culture. There may not be any incentive to address issues outside of staff members' assigned duties. To meet the goal of libraries working toward an equitable society means not only creating and maintaining inclusive organizations, but also interrogating practices and procedures with attention to marginalized groups. Connecting daily work directly with the missions of library organizations better allows librarians to leverage the diversity in their organizations, establishing the library as a change agent within their communities and broader society.

Addressing Fragility and Microaggressions

Librarians and library organizations must become comfortable with being uncomfortable. Even in mission-focused organizations with a high degree of self-awareness, conversations about diversity and inclusion are often more fraught than other discussions. Organizational leaders must consider why discussions about systemic oppression can be highly emotional and personal. Leaders must equip themselves with tools and strategies to enter into these conversations and drive them forward. Consider the range of conversations about how personal lives affect work that occur daily in the library, while conversations touching on diversity, inclusion, or oppression do not occur in the same frequency. The barriers to conversations about systemic oppression and its effects are not based on discomfort with having hard conversations, but rather based on resistance to talking about these specific topics.

Intersectional conversations are a third rail because of the personal and emotional positions each of us have in the systems of oppression and the discomfort with addressing those positions, especially in a mixed group. Members of underrepresented groups face a work environment typified by microaggressions, where experiences are neither heard nor valued. Members of majority groups are often unpracticed in confronting the realities of racial and other oppressions. As Robin DiAngelo describes, they "have not had to build the cognitive or affective skills or develop the stamina that would allow for constructive engagement."[21]

When members of marginalized groups consider forwarding intersectional conversations, they face a seemingly insurmountable wall. The conversation is too big and it is often derailed before it is properly addressed. It is challenging to sum up a lifetime of experience in a way that is meaningful to colleagues who may be unaware that a problem even exists. As a recent study by Jaena Alabi indicates, "non-minority academic librarians do not recognize racial microaggressions that their minority colleagues could be experiencing."[22] At the same time, members of marginalized groups are burdened with the task of taking on additional roles related to diversity. Damasco and Hodges studied faculty librarians and found that over half of minority respondents in their study felt "pressured into engaging in diversity-related service activities."[23] Minority librarians have hidden workloads and often manage diversity work in addition to other faculty duties while "white colleagues are not burdened by the same expectations."[24] Roughly a third of faculty librarians of color felt that they could not freely voice their opinion, while around forty percent felt that they were excluded from informal networks in their libraries.[25] Additional pressures and demands resulted in high levels of job stress, early burnout, and lower retention for minority librarians.[26] Until microaggressions in the workplace are addressed, a hostile, exclusive work environment will remain and the diversity of librarianship will continue to suffer. Recognizing the realities of the workplace for librarians from marginalized groups is the first step

---

21 Robin DiAngelo, "White Fragility," *International Journal of Critical Pedagogy* 3, no. 3 (2011): 57.

22 Jaena Alabi, "Racial Microaggressions in Academic Libraries: Results Of A Survey Of Minority And Non-Minority Librarians," *Journal of Academic Librarianship* 41 (2015): 51.

23 Ione T Damasco and Dracine Hodges, "Tenure and Promotion Experiences of Academic Librarians of Color," *College & Research Libraries* 73, no. 3 (2012): 291.

24 Ibid., 298.

25 Ibid., 296.

26 Alabi, "Racial Microagressions" 47; Damasco and Hodges, "Tenure and Promotion Experiences," 298.

in addressing them and creating a safe space to begin meaningful conversations about approaches to diversity, inclusion, and systemic oppression.

When members of dominant groups confront the oppression of the minority, their ability to engage is hampered by social factors that protect the dominant status as normative. Robin DiAngelo describes the result of social structures that protect white people from race-based stress as White Fragility, "the insulated environment of racial protection [that] builds white expectations for racial comfort while at the same time lowering the ability to tolerate racial stress."[27] When faced with almost any level of racial stress, fragility triggers interruptions and counter-moves to shut down the conversation and defer responsibility.[28] However, DiAngelo suggests "viewing white anger, defensiveness, silence, and withdrawal in response to issues of race through the framework of White Fragility may help frame the problem as an issue of stamina-building, and thereby guide our interventions accordingly."[29] While there are important differences between specific oppressions, the framework of fragility has been applied to other privileged groups in society. Organizational leaders need to understand their own fragility in regard to their privilege(s) in order to "build the stamina to sustain conscious and explicit engagement."[30] Learning to confront one's own fragility is useful in developing the capacity for engagement with others.

Organizations need to provide resources to address barriers to engagement for both members of marginalized groups and members of dominant groups. Organizations should focus on providing concrete support for members of marginalized groups and requiring involvement from members of dominant groups. To support members of marginalized groups, leaders need to publicly recognize the experiences and knowledge of members of marginalized groups at various levels of the organization. Leaders need to develop scaffolding in their organizations to support librarians and library staff as they develop the stamina to engage in intersectional conversations. By creating opportunities for members of

---

27 DiAngelo, "White Fragility," 54.

28 Ibid., 57.

29 Ibid., 67.

30 Ibid., 66.

dominant groups to confront their fragility and marginalized groups to speak their truth in a low stakes environment, the organization can facilitate the development of skills necessary to address systemic oppression and create an inclusive culture.

Addressing Our Shit

To lead intersectional conversations, leaders need to demonstrate authenticity and be prepared to guide others in the work required. Leaders can begin by examining their reactions to microaggressions and to their fragilities. Investigating internalized oppressions and motivations for opposing and dismantling systemic oppression is also essential. Self-examination is a lifetime of work, but is critical to successfully engaging in and leading anti-oppression work. Academic librarians exist within an academy that is dominated by straight, Christian, white men. From collegiality to professionalism, marginalized people are pressured by the academy to conform to the ideal of what "an academic" looks like. In academic culture, modes of communication and knowledge outside those of academia are not recognized nor valued. Acceptance into the current culture of academic libraries requires marginalized persons to "perform whiteness," which expends time and energy to "conceal their authentic selves in the interest of survival."[31] Negotiating an identity that is authentic to experiences and background may entail embracing identities and characteristics that inherently challenge the culture of academia. Pushing too hard against the culture can be detrimental to personal success.[32] Maintaining a balance is an ongoing struggle, but one that requires conscious engagement.

In writing this chapter, the authors had to confront the ways we avoid intersectional conversations, and our complicity in the absence of these conversations. In spite of knowing that microaggressions and forceful shutdowns of conversations exist, we still do not want to step outside the comfort zone of our traditional library work to intervene when they occur. Members of marginalized groups are often called

---

31 Galvan, "Soliciting Performance, Hiding Bias."

32 April Hathcock, "White Librarianship in Blackface: Diversity Initiatives In LIS." *In The Library With The Lead Pipe*, October 7, 2015. http://www.inthelibrarywiththeleadpipe.org/2015/lis-diversity/.

upon in libraries and across campus to provide input and advice on diversity related issues, and can experience advocacy fatigue. The authors acknowledge that we would benefit from introspection and reflection. Our willingness to educate our co-workers when the opportunities arise is counterbalanced by some resentment that we, the underrepresented, are expected to take on this responsibility in addition to other library duties.

SELF-CARE AND SUPPORT

Taking up anti-oppression work in our organizations is heavy work. To sustain the work we must pay attention to sustaining ourselves. We need to be prepared to define our limits about when and how we can be visible leaders in areas in which we are not experts. We should also allow some flexibility for ourselves and our colleagues. This is not a universal opt-out, but we should be attentive to our need and especially the need of colleagues from marginalized groups to protect themselves from the heavy toll these conversations can take.

We can challenge each other to further develop our frameworks of understanding, learn new tools and techniques, and receive mentoring from other marginalized people both in doing the work of anti-oppression and in succeeding in our professional careers. Cultivating safe spaces in the profession for those involved in anti-oppression work is essential. Safe spaces provide opportunities to practice intersectional conversations. We can become comfortable with addressing difficult topics by learning what resonates in these conversations. Safe spaces allow us to express our frustrations and celebrations without fear of being misunderstood. Progress can be marked; changes can be seen and recognized. Individual growth and development happen in safe spaces in ways that may not occur in our everyday work environments.

LEADING THE WAY FORWARD

There are no universal solutions to the challenges discussed in this chapter. This is a complex organizational issue involving many forms of diversity. Leaders can recognize the individual contexts and lived experience of each person and draw on that as a point of strength in the organization. Libraries need to design practices and processes in advance that address how we speak, how we think, and what we do in an atmosphere that is respectful and open to change.

Our intersectionalities offer coalitions and points of leverage. Leaders can begin by connecting their intersectional personal journeys to their professional identities and values. As Kimberle Crenshaw states, "it may be easier for us to understand the need for and to summon the courage to challenge groups that are after all, in one sense, "home" to us, in the name of the parts of us that are not made at home."[33] From our "home" in the library community, members of marginalized groups can bring challenges from their other identities. Indeed, using the language and approaches of librarianship can help us communicate these challenges most effectively. Leaders who typify both the ideals and the characteristics of the organization are most effective.[34] Leaders can develop and identify their personal approach as an intersectional librarian in line with core values of librarianship, encouraging that approach to spread through their organizations.

Even if intersectional conversations are fumbling and difficult to "get right," it is essential to have them. Every opportunity is another chance to learn from the last encounter and build on past successes. Having uncomfortable discussions will build tolerance and develop intellectual and emotional version of "muscle memory." Even with commitment, training and reading, leaders and librarians will not be ready for the difficulty of intersectional conversations—it takes stamina and fortitude to effect change. As leaders, we may not have the skills or expertise to lead these conversations. If necessary, we must seek out experts for help.

It is important for libraries to have strategic goals and diversity initiatives in place, however, small efforts can have big impacts. Leading the way forward presents opportunities in the organization for individuals to lead where they are. Individuals who act inclusively send a message of inclusion that can draw out others. Organizations need to create a culture of understanding and accountability to address the emotional reactions and microaggressions that can occur during these conversations. Leaders can set clear expectations of acceptable

---

33 Kimberle Crenshaw, "Mapping the Margins: Intersectionality, Identity Politics, and Violence against Women of Color," *Stanford Law Review* 43, no. 6 (1991): 1299.

34 Stephen D. Reicher, Alexander S. Haslam, and Michael J. Platow, "The New Psychology Of Leadership," *Scientific American* 18, no. 4 (2007): 22-29.

and unacceptable behavior, helping to expand the range of safe spaces that are needed for these conversations. The library is a microcosm of the broader environment: the campus and the community. When identifying and seeking out support and expertise, leaders should broaden their scope beyond the library both in their local and professional environments. The Association of College and Research Libraries (ACRL) provides eleven standards on cultural competency and provides a framework to "support libraries in engaging the complexities of providing services to diverse populations, and recruiting and maintaining a diverse library workforce."[35] Focusing on cultural competency, organizational and professional values, cross-cultural knowledge and skills, workforce diversity, and inclusion provides a pathway for intersectional conversations, interactions, and possibility of change.

CONCLUSION

The growing range and depth of theoretical and practical research on diversity and inclusion in libraries is heartening. As significant research emerges from other fields, intersectional librarians will do well to continue to seek that research out and translate the findings into the library context. Bringing research from other fields into a library-specific context will encourage more members of the profession to engage with these ideas and their applications. Drawing organizational change research together with research on microaggressions and fragility will be useful in guiding conversations forward.

In addition to the dissemination of research and theory from other fields, the authors noted several areas where additional library research would be useful in conducting intersectional conversations. Research examining how libraries create strategic goals related to diversity and inclusion, as well as how libraries enact, assess, and improve those goals will provide guidance as intersectional leaders focus on developing inclusive organizations. Effective strategies drawn from best practices are essential to share in the professional literature. Useful areas to share best practices include career support for members

---

35 Association of College and Research Libraries, "Diversity Standards: Cultural Competency for Academic Libraries (2012)." Accessed September 1, 2016. http://www.ala.org/acrl/standards/diversity.

of marginalized groups; sustainable diversity work; responses to white fragility; developing systems analysis and awareness in library contexts; and inclusive organizational planning in libraries.

Engaging in the work of diversity, inclusion, and anti-oppression in our profession, our organizations, and our communities is a heavy and deep commitment. The work is emotional and draining, taking a toll not only intellectually, but also physically and spiritually. Change happens in small increments; long-term progress is difficult to see from our standpoint on the ground. The success of this work is measured over generations. Leaders will continue to build on past initiatives, adapting them to better serve current climates. To sustain themselves and the work, leaders must develop identities which integrate their intersectionalities into their professional identities, so that intersectional conversations can occur naturally. Through writing this article, the authors have recommitted to engaging in forwarding intersectional conversations, and are encouraged that we will not be the only ones stepping up to the call for action. As crucial as it is to make our profession more open to intersectional conversations about diversity, inclusion, and oppression, we must recognize that this work is very difficult. We take it on because we are invested not only in making the work of our profession meaningful, but because we believe that the work is for the greater good.

Bibliography

Alabi, Jaena. 2015. "Racial Microaggressions in Academic Libraries: Results of a Survey f Minority and Non-Minority Librarians." *Journal of Academic Librarianship* 41, no. 1 (2015): 47-51.

American Library Association. "ALA Demographics Studies." August 27, 2016. http://www.ala.org/research/sites/ala. org.research/files/content/initiatives/membershipsurveys/ September2014ALADemographics.pdf.

————. "American Library Association Strategic Directions." Accessed August 27, 2016. http://www.ala.org/aboutala/ sites/ala.org.aboutala/files/content/governance/StrategicPlan/ Strategic%20Directions%20June%2028%202015.pdf.

————. "Diversity Counts 2012 Tables." Accessed August 27, 2016. http://www.ala.org/offices/sites/ala.org.offices/files/content/ diversity/diversitycounts/diversitycountstables2012.pdf

————. "Diversity, Equity, and Inclusion." Accessed June 13, 2016. http://www.ala.org/advocacy/diversity.

————. "Recruiting for Diversity." Accessed August 27, 2016. http://www.ala.org/advocacy/diversity/workforcedevelopment/ recruitmentfordiversity.

Association of College and Research Libraries. "Diversity Standards: Cultural Competency forAcademic Libraries (2012)." Accessed September 1, 2016. http://www.ala.org/acrl/standards/diversity.

Brook, Freeda, Dave Ellenwood, and Althea Eannace Lazzaro. "In Pursuit of Antiracist Social Justice: Denaturalizing Whiteness in the Academic Library." *Library Trends* 64, no. 2 (2015): 246-284.

Crenshaw, Kimberle. "Mapping the Margins: Intersectionality, Identity Politics, and Violence against Women of Color." *Stanford Law Review* 43, no. 6 (1991):1241-1299.

Damasco, Ione T, and Dracine Hodges."Tenure and Promotion Experiences of Academic Librarians of Color." *College & Research Libraries* 73, no. 3 (2012): 279-301.

DiAngelo, Robin. "White Fragility." *International Journal of Critical Pedagogy* 3, no. 3 (2011): 54-70.

Galvan, Angela. "Soliciting Performance, Hiding Bias: Whiteness and Librarianship." *In The Library With The Lead Pipe,* June 3, 2015. http://www.inthelibrarywiththeleadpipe.org/2015/soliciting-performance-hiding-bias-whiteness-and-librarianship/.

Halvorson, Heidi Grant, and David Rock. "Beyond Bias: Neuroscience Research Shows How New Organizational Practices Can Shift Ingrained Thinking." *strategy + business,* July 13, 2015. Accessed November 22, 2016. http://www.strategy-business.com/article/00345

Hathcock, April. "White Librarianship in Blackface: Diversity Initiatives In LIS." *In The Library With The Lead Pipe,* October 7, 2015. http://www.inthelibrarywiththeleadpipe.org/2015/lis-diversity/.

Morales, Myrna, Em Claire Knowles, and Chris Bourg. "Diversity, Social Justice, and the Future of Libraries." *portal: Libraries and the Academy* 14, no. 3 (2015): 439-451.

OED Online, September 2016, s.v. "diversity."

OED Online, September 2016, s.v. "inclusiveness."

Phillips, Katherine W. "How Diversity Makes Us Smarter: Being Around People Who Are Different From Us Makes Us More Creative, More Diligent And Harder-Working." *Scientific American*, October 1, 2014. Accessed November 22, 2016. http://www.scientificamerican.com/article/how-diversity-makes-us-smarter/.

Race Forward / The Center for Racial Justice Innovation. 2014. "About Race Forward." Accessed October 10, 2016. https://www.raceforward.org/about.

————. "Moving The Race Conversation Forward: How The Media Covers Racism, And Other Barriers To Productive Racial Discourse: Part 1," 3-4. Accessed August 27, 2016. https://www.raceforward.org/research/reports/moving-race-conversation-forward.

Reicher, Stephen D., Alexander S. Haslam, and Michael J. Platow. "The New Psychology Of Leadership." *Scientific American* 18, no. 4 (2007): 22-29.

Vinopal, Jennifer."The Quest for Diversity in Library Staffing: From Awareness to Action." *In the Library with the Lead Pipe*, January 13, 2016. http://www.inthelibrarywiththeleadpipe.org/2016/quest-for-diversity/.

ONE LIBRARY, TWO CULTURES

Dale Askey and Jennifer Askey

In many libraries it is axiomatic to speak of two cultures coexisting uncomfortably: the familiar "library culture," which exists in areas performing primarily traditional work, and the "new," disruptive culture of library IT. We see clear evidence of this divide in many places. In a recent Ithaka S+R issue brief, an academic library director "bemoaned the clashes associated with bringing 'people who do not share the culture and values' who nevertheless wish to drive decision-making in the library." In order to avoid these clashes, the director mused whether "the library would be better served by 'buying' services from campus IT with a strong service-level agreement."[1] This instrumental and reductionist view of IT—it is a set of concrete deliverables one can simply buy, not fibre in the organization's fabric—is not unique to this director nor uncommon in libraries of various sizes. In the past few years, we have seen a library as large as the University of British Columbia move nearly all of its IT staff and functions to central university IT. The core issue with this mindset is that it continues to posit the library as being about services and collections, ignoring the obvious shift that has made these two core functions interwoven with and driven by increasingly sophisticated technologies.

By musing about outsourcing IT to another campus unit—setting aside for the moment actually doing it—the director quoted in the Ithaka report is repeating a common refrain in libraries, namely,

---

1 Roger Schonfeld, "Organizing the Work of the Research Library," Ithaka S+R, August 18, 2016, doi: 10.18665/sr.283717.

that IT work and library work belong in two separate categories, with overlap only occurring when it comes time to implement the technology. This mindset excludes the possibility that "library work" has become itself highly technical in nature and that librarian knowledge and IT have become inseparable. For many library staff, certainly those working in or in close proximity to technical work, this inseparability is not questioned. Yet many library leaders bring a perspective from an earlier automation generation, before Web and other technologies massively disrupted user expectations of libraries, and have never worked in a technology role. For many, IT remains a foreign body, typically viewed in instrumental terms. This mindset also results in an emphasis on traditional library services to a degree that serves neither the library nor its users in the academic landscape of today or tomorrow. This, in turn, affects the recruitment of people with different knowledge and skill sets to our detriment.

Frequent attempts to bridge the divide between traditional and new library work frame the issue as being primarily one of competing priorities. In a typical scenario, those on the library side perceive the IT staff as inflexible and rigid, while those in IT lament their exclusion from broader library planning and initiatives because they are not "librarians" (even though some are). In the era when library IT departments comprised a small cohort within the academic library system, this chasm between the two silos and the resulting misunderstanding or devaluing of the other group's priorities may have seemed unavoidable, as professionals engaged in library work sought to protect the status quo in the face of technological change. However, the mission of the library is changing and that change is altering the nature of library IT work and its role within the institution. With this shift and this work in mind, we are compelled to examine the professional discourse around technology in libraries and specifically to explore the gendered nature of this increasingly prominent IT element.

From the library IT vantage point, many of us have watched outbursts of bad behavior in the broader IT sector (#Gamergate[2] is a prominent example) and perhaps felt self-congratulatory for being in far more diverse and tolerant organizations. Yet while we have

2 Gamergate is a name applied to a set of events in 2014 where a number of female game developers and social critics received severe abuse, including death threats, from men in the larger gaming community. It has become a shorthand way to refer to endemic sexism in broader tech communities.

typically not seen such openly hostile vitriol directed at women or minorities in our IT departments, a quick glance around the room at any library technology event will make clear that we have little to tout in terms of being more diverse or welcoming. While great strides have been made in recent years at conferences such as code4lib, Digital Library Federation, and others to include more women, progress at events has not translated into major changes in our libraries. Certainly, if we identify the technically oriented positions in our organizations, it would be hard for any of us to assert that we have achieved diversity reflective of the broader communities. Our role and position within the academy, a locus of open discourse, if not perfect policies on gender, sexuality, and race, means that we are vigilant about the more egregious and identifiable forms of discrimination. However, this does not guarantee that we are equally vigilant toward the subtler, yet perhaps even more pervasive and pernicious forms of discrimination and bias.

A portion of what has animated academic libraries' attitudes toward inclusion and diversity can possibly be found in the traditional (and current) demographics of librarians themselves. Women are and have been a majority in the profession. But perhaps we have mistaken the presence of women in our organizations, certainly the presence of women in leadership roles, as evidence of two accomplishments. First, we assume that we are more egalitarian because we are not male-dominated, as the rest of academia tends to be. Second, many take for granted that the presence of women in leadership roles means that libraries benefit from leadership from a feminist perspective. Clearly, this is not the case, or else there would be no reason to write this chapter, nor produce this volume. Simply because libraries are a female-dominated industry, does not mean that libraries are feminist workplaces.

We argue that, rather than feminist, the work and organization of academic libraries is feminized. In her discussion of librarianship as a feminized profession, Roxanne Shirazi notes that "[t]he idea of a feminized profession is part of the larger idea of a sexual division of labor, an occupational stratification based on one's gender presentation."[3] Analogous to the caring professions we traditionally

---

3 Roxanne Shirazi, "Reproducing the Academy: Librarians and the Question of Service in the Digital Humanities," (blog), July 15, 2014, https://roxanneshirazi.com/2014/07/15/reproducing-the-academy-librarians-and-the-question-of-service-in-the-digital-humanities/.

associate with feminized work, the library profession has traditionally been characterized as requiring not only a soft voice, but a soft skill set, including eagerness to help others complete work, find resources, or empower themselves with information. Shirazi examines the fraught relationship of librarians to digital humanities support—closely related to library technology both by nature and organizational positioning—by noting that feminized work is characterized by notions of service and emotional labor, which tend to relocate this work to a supporting role because it is associated with "little tangible productivity measures but... requires workers to appear as though they love their job."[4] This mirrors the assertions of some library leaders, such as those represented in the Ithaka report, who see the fundamental work of the library as that of supporting research and discovery, rather than collaborating directly within those enterprises. Applied to the dynamic at play in libraries between (largely female) library staff and (largely male, perhaps even external) IT staff, the stark cultural difference comes all the more to the fore. The former group assesses the need, makes the case, secures the resources, organizes the meetings, and solicits and analyzes user feedback, while the latter group is left to work within the protected—often quite literally, in a locked or inaccessible space—bubble of systems and coding, freed from people-oriented tasks. To assert that this clearly reflects a gendered dynamic is not challenging. Even the phrase "IT guys" provides evidence of this negative gendered interplay at work. In most libraries, there are men working as library staff and women in IT areas, but close observation of the expectations these individuals face within their cohorts will often underscore how we assign work and set expectations based on this underlying gendered conceptualization of emotional versus technical work.

Given the gender dynamic in play as it relates to specific kinds of work, assessing diversity in libraries by looking at staffing numbers doesn't provide a real indication of the gendered nature of library work. While the overall organization skews toward the norm, with a majority of employees being women, the further one moves across the organizational chart toward IT roles, the staff becomes distinctly male. The temptation exists to characterize this as exclusively a staffing problem, i.e. if we just put more women into the mix (or people of

---

4 Ibid.

color, or members of another identified minority group), the "diversity problem" would solve itself. We should by now be wary of this numbers approach, as it reflects facile and glib approaches to diversity on many academic campuses, where we congratulate ourselves for hiring transgender, queer, and/or people of color into faculty roles, while at the same time ignoring the lack of such representation in the ranks of senior faculty and in the higher administration. This lack of diverse leadership across most campuses, not only in their libraries, exists despite awareness of the problem and inclusion of diversity statements in job postings. Thus, we posit that promoting real and meaningful diversity in library IT divisions is not simply a matter of hiring a more diverse employee cohort, but rather one of institutional vision and priorities, where diversity is represented in the leadership, staffing, vision making, and research profile of the library.

Beginning with the assertion that traditional library work is feminized work, in what follows we explore the discursive divisions between IT culture and the library workplace in order to elucidate the gendered ramifications of the service mentality within academic libraries. Following that, we explore the agenda of the library as an instrument of cultural conservation and how the library's proclamations of itself as a neutral repository of information are inaccurate. As a conservative institution libraries replicate, to a certain extent, the libraries of the past, instead of looking forward to the needs of library users and workers of the future. As a way to conceptualize how diversity and the work of the academy intertwine, we turned to Audre Lorde's seminal essay, "The Master's Tools Will Never Dismantle the Master's House."[5] In this speech, given at a women's conference, Lorde exhorted her feminist colleagues to turn difference into strength. Anticipating some of the larger discursive trends in third-wave feminism, Lorde reminds her feminist peers that "women of today are still being called upon... to educate men as to our existence and our needs" and draws a parallel between that phenomenon and the way black feminists of her generation were being marginalized by their white peers.[6] Rejecting what we would now refer to as tokenism, Lorde demands that the feminist movement use

---

5 Audre Lorde, "The Master's Tools Will Never Dismantle the Master's House," in *Sister Outsider* (Berkeley: Crossing Press, 1984), 110-113.

6 Ibid., 113.

different methods, a different lens, and a different set of tools to create a different culture. Similarly, when thinking about the implications of feminist library leadership on digital culture in the library, we suggest that the methods and tools employed in library work need to change and, at the same time, the work libraries do needs to change as well. Rather than parachuting diversity into our institutions via targeted hires or special projects, what if intersectional feminism and inclusion of diverse viewpoints became the mode of operations for academic libraries? Would new tools, deployed on localized and embodied collections, projects, and practices, help create a new house, in which staff and librarians would represent and reflect the communities they serve? We suggest possibilities for changing the work of the library— bringing traditional services and emergent, technology-rich projects into productive dialogue—in a way that not only solidifies the relevance of the academic library in the future, but also diversifies the notion of library work and the culture libraries wish to preserve. As minority and marginalized populations have argued, representation in culture makes a difference. Seeing the experiences, values, community and interests of feminists, people of color, the LGBQT+ community reflected in the active work and the public face of the library will, we argue, do more to diversify the staff within the library than equal opportunity statements.

Libraries as Feminized Workplaces and Library IT

To be clear, parallels do exist between library IT culture and the broader IT culture, perhaps inevitably so because people can move between the two spheres and both define roles similarly, e.g. a system administrator occupies a fairly defined work niche regardless of the broader organization. As such, some of the dynamics that play out in IT workplaces manifest themselves in a variety of ways in the library workplace, ranging from superficial aspects such as office decor to more potent elements such as an over-reliance on jargon and the associated creation of an insider culture.

There are also some practical characteristics of IT work that contrast markedly with broader academic library culture. The acceptance of telecommuting arrangements is a notable example. Similarly, the organizing principle of most libraries is to devolve a great deal of decision making to teams, committees, working groups, and task forces, i.e. to identify something that needs to be done and assign it out to one of these groups. In an IT environment, the task would have a project manager, and be conducted according to fairly rigid and standardized project management principles. Library professionals tend to prefer collaborative, committee-based decision making processes in groups, whereas IT professionals utilize a project management environment where tasks are delegated to groups and, frequently, the "scrum master" coordinates various components and shepherds them to completion.

Many people engaged in library IT work are keenly aware of these divergences in work culture and history and seek ways to bridge the gap. The resonance that the Ada Initiative found in libraries reflects that general phenomenon. The Ada Initiative existed between 2011 and 2015 and arose in response to the barriers and discrimination women face when working in IT. Many library IT leaders—the majority of whom are still men—embraced the Ada Initiative. With its emphasis on training and visibility, however, the Ada Initiative's efforts also fell into the category of the numbers game: highlighting barriers and aiming to increase the number of women in jobs in the technology sector.

Yet despite the Ada Initiative and the efforts of some library IT managers, gaps in diversity and differences in culture between library IT and academic libraries at large remain visible to anyone willing to cast a critical eye. We would like to suggest that these gaps exist at the foundational level and can be traced to the arguably feminized nature of much traditional library work—providing service, promoting faculty relations, and engaging in student instruction. These activities are laudable extensions of the library into campus culture, but also serve to position librarians in their own eyes, as well as in the eyes of their institutions, as "mere" service providers. The notion of librarians as support staff or service providers to those who do the "real" work of the university—professors and, secondarily, students—reinforces our tacit comprehension of library work as gendered and feminine. Faculty relations, instruction, and reference support are the customer service of the libraries and associated with them is a sense not of rigor or research, but rather of emotional labor and handholding.

Accepting the role of the academic library as one of assistance or support conforms to "traditional" expectations around librarians and librarianship. At the same time that some areas of the library are expanding their scope and mission, adding publishing platforms, digital research labs, and makerspaces, much of the work of the traditional library continues to rest firmly within the parameters of the helping professions, rather than the researching professions. We would suggest that greater attention to the opportunities afforded by the technological turn in libraries can offer colleagues across all departments of the academic library increased agency in their work, as well as in the research enterprise of the academy.

This notion of libraries and librarians as assistants to the larger academic research enterprise extends to and is reinforced by the software that most librarians use in their regular line of work. ILS interfaces and cataloging software reward unquestioning engagement with and commitment to working with the tools as they exist. Concurrently, these software packages penalize users for questioning workflows, attempting customization, or demanding transparency and collaboration in the creation of these tools. The corporations behind library software approach library professionals and their work paternalistically, removing any opportunity for professionals to bring their local expertise to bear on the design or implementation of the core tools of the trade. This technical arrangement essentially feminizes entire categories of librarianship, demanding that professionals working with these platforms defer their intellects and their professional curiosity to a commercial entity whose primary goal is to turn a profit by selling supposedly essential tools that, in fact, undermine autonomy and creativity within the profession they claim to serve. The parallels here to the creation of computers and operating systems as "black boxes" where the magic of computation happens and to which we, as users have little or no access, are apparent. And, as Wendy Chun has shown, the transition of computation from a physical, embodied job to an electronic, microscopic, digital job brought with it the decline and erasure of women, people of color, and the working classes from the history of computing.[7] The relationship between the working professional and her tools can be an empowering one. The relationship between the librarian and the software she works with is not.

---

7 Wendy Hui Kyong Chun, "On Sorcery and Source Codes," in *Programmed Visions: Software and Memory* (Boston: MIT Press, 2011), 19-54, 29.

This situation in the library leaves most librarians in a position akin to cogs in a machine, rather than independent, professional, and capable researchers, information specialists, subject-area experts, and the like. This situation also draws our attention to the relationship between the professional, the tool, the workflow, and the product in our examination of IT culture in academic libraries. If, as we posit, part of the problem of a lack of diversity in libraries is the traditional perception of librarianship and the library as a whole as a site of feminized work, then instead of looking at the people in these jobs as the solution to the problem, we can look at the nature of the job itself and examine whether there is opportunity to shift the nature of the work from passive and supportive to active and generative.

We are suggesting this examination not only because we are interested in and committed to diversity of all kinds within our organizations, but because to examine this landscape and explore possible changes in library jobs presents us with a real opportunity to participate in the creation of tomorrow's academic library. Such a library is a place of diversity, encompassing multiple knowledges and ways of knowing, striving for historical accuracy and social justice; in sum, a workplace defined by an intersectional feminist perspective. However, our current staffing decisions, library workflow patterns, and engagement with standard library software promote the recreation of tomorrow's academic library in the image of today's academic library. While myriad articles and experts across the academy insist that the nature of research, publishing, teaching, and learning is changing in response to the digital turn, to the economic downturn, and to demographic changes in university student populations, the work of the academic library has changed little. Asking today's library to create the personnel, service, and research diversity that our institutions and our world need is unrealistic.

Replicating Ourselves

Nearly every academic library, large or small, takes pride in their special collections, the rare and unique items that they possess. We compete with each other to secure significant gifts, often offering generous purchase terms and/or assuming extensive and costly processing work without receiving any funds from the donor. Once we have secured the collections, we hold celebrations and issue press releases. Having expended such effort and gone to such lengths, we then make a virtue of holding these collections, whether or not they actually fit the profile and history of the university. (For example, McMaster University holds the papers of Bertrand Russell, although Russell had little to do with McMaster or Canada.) The trouble with this is that given the demographics of academic workers over the past century, the vast majority of these marquee collections stem from white, heterosexual men who dominated most academic disciplines or held prominent positions in society. This puts libraries in the role of championing, even reifying, canonical notions of scholarship and research, as well as serving a patriarchial agenda. While we typically have at least some holdings from members of underrepresented groups, these collections are much smaller and less comprehensive. We tend not to single them out in the same way that we tout the papers of well-known male figures. Inspecting the "Collection Highlights" segment of Yale's Beinecke Rare Book & Manuscript Library's website, one must click through to the third page (twelve collections per page) to hit the first collection by a woman, for example (Edith Wharton).[8] This is not an exceptional experience.

Despite a history of claiming libraries as neutral repositories, our collections, in particular our special collections, push a culturally biased agenda. Chris Bourg and Bess Sadler distill much of our current discontent with the library as repository of culture, and confronted this legacy directly in a 2015 essay in the *Code4Lib Journal*, opening with the blunt statement that "[i]n spite of the pride many libraries take in their neutrality, libraries have never been neutral repositories of knowledge."[9] Significantly, Bourg and Sadler take their argument past situating this flaw solely in our collections and note that our practices also tend to replicate "societal patterns of exclusion and inequality."[10] This is not only the case with long-established practices such as cataloging, they assert, but continues with newer form of work entering libraries, such as the

---

8 "Collection Highlights," accessed April 13, 2016, http://beinecke.library.yale.edu/collections/highlights.

9 Bess Sadler and Chris Bourg, "Feminism and the Future of Library Discovery," *Code4Lib Journal* 28 (April 15, 2015), http://journal.code4lib.org/articles/10425.

10 Ibid.

creation of software tools. If the day-to-day work of the library, the work that engages both the librarians and the users, replicates the dominant social patterns of inclusion and exclusion, then libraries, as institutions, are not doing what they could in terms of becoming diverse and inclusive organizations and supporting diversity and inclusion across campuses and research agendas.

We suggest an extension of Bourg and Sadler's argument, which covers the implications of feminist theory for human-computer interaction, to an examination of the ways in which libraries pursue their mission. For the nature of the library's mission can attract or repel diverse groups in terms of work and in terms of the profession as a whole. While libraries often have mission statements that explain why we exist, these statements leave uncontested the notion that the library is a repository and conservator of canonical epistemes. Libraries reify the ways that librarians—people who have chosen to work in libraries—conceptualize libraries and where they place them within the academic experience.

The library of yesterday can't serve the university of today. Continuing to insist on the primacy of collections and the importance of cataloging at the expense, say, of digitization projects, digital scholarship centers, makerspaces, open data initiatives, or high-speed computing facilities may well translate into decreased interest on the part of our communities in what we have to offer. Additionally, by continuing to allow outside vendors and established tools and processes to dictate our workflow, we may also run the risk of becoming peripheral to the research and teaching agenda of our universities. For, as research and teaching demand more interaction, more computing power, more problem-based learning, more hands-on research even in the humanities and social sciences, traditional library instruction and reference services will not be able to meet the needs of the campus. The current situation, in which library work is conceptualized as feminized service work, represents an external problem in terms of libraries' relevance to their communities, as well as an internal problem in terms of the attractiveness of library work to diverse groups of employees. By consigning the library to being the helpmate of the academic enterprise, today's library professionals may well turn off the type of students, researchers, scholars, coders, builders, or makers who would be able to serve a new academic population.

There is no "digital library;" there is only the library

By bringing an intersectional feminist view to bear on the issues outlined above, we hope to create a framework both for understanding where we are as well as outlining new ways forward. We need to establish a path toward bringing the two cultures, library and IT, into harmony with each other, eliminating what we perceive to be false divisions.

We cannot persist with our current ways of doing things. More effort and more discussion will not resolve our lingering issues nor show us the way out of the cul-de-sac. In particular, if library leaders continue to insist on a division between library work and IT work and generally reject deeper, more critical engagement with technical work, we would continue with the feminized—and increasingly marginalized—support and service roles of the traditional library that risk becoming increasingly irrelevant to our uses. Moreover, as library work becomes more dependent on technology, this division means that library and campus administrators may view this work as something that can be excised from the library and outsourced to another campus entity or third party. This leads to multiple critical failures. For one, it fractures lines of communication that should exist between any part of the library with a stake in the outcomes of a project involving technology. It also creates significant logistical challenges; the library becomes just another client for those external parties, who prioritize their work based on their own perceptions of criticality, which will likely not favor libraries. Not least, given the well documented diversity issues in broader IT culture, we would essentially be outsourcing work to an environment that is notoriously hostile to diversity and seemingly incapable of unseating its current dominant culture.

Countering the divisive mindset, feminist library technology politics acknowledges the non-neutrality of knowledge and establishes practices not only to dismantle entrenched systems of marginalization and oppression, but also to build up a knowledge and technology economy within the library that represents multiple epistemes and encourages knowledge production for the 21st century. We suggest that this will not happen through established diversity measures that seek to "fix" gender and racial imbalances in libraries through targeted hiring. Rather, it requires critical examination of the work we do in libraries. This is how we create new tools.

One of the endemic disadvantages of a library bifurcated along the lines of library and IT cultures is that as we create these new tools, we are doing so in an environment that perpetuates the worst tendencies of both cultures by failing to create meaningful dialogue and interaction between those who know the collections and have extensive relationships with students and faculty, on the one hand, and those with the ability to create tools using coding and other technology skills. Put somewhat differently, it denies those from the library side access to learning about how to do the hands-on work of tool creation, as well as simultaneously denying those in the IT camp any possible competence when it comes to offering insights and suggestions for how the work of the library could take shape. Instead, the library side creates what in software development terms would be functional requirements—although these desires are often neither detailed nor explained but rather more typically expressed as "we need this"—and passes them to the IT side where the developers work in a partial vacuum when it comes to parsing context or influencing the requirements. While this is not the universal paradigm in academic libraries, it will sound fairly familiar to many.

What we need instead is to emphasize tool creation that acknowledges the local context, work, and collections that reflect the community's makeup and values. We can diversify our staff if we diversify our work. At present, we are rather myopic in our approach to tool creation, often framing our work in terms of competition with entities outside the academy, primarily Google. The discovery layer is our answer to Google's various search platforms; similarly, we promote our institutional repository as an alternative scholarly distribution mode to academic journals. Instead, we should seek to foster projects that elicit and address the needs of our community.

Given this, it is not surprising that we have major challenges solving two interconnected issues: recruiting and retaining a truly diverse workforce and bringing the two cultures in our walls into harmony. By changing the work we prioritize and shifting the emphasis away from the patriarchal legacy toward a more inclusive view of collections and their users, we stand a better chance of creating meaningful diversity in our libraries. By building a more diverse workforce and then—and this is the essential message we should be hearing—actually giving them the space and authority to shape their work, we can begin to close the gap between the two cultures as well as build sustained, meaningful diversity.

We are beginning to see evidence of a new paradigm emerging. The evolution of the Code4Lib community serves as a bellwether for the path that we are hopefully following. As with many technically oriented groups, in its earlier years it was a small and largely male dominated community, yet as early as 2008, annual conference organizers began offering gender and diversity scholarships.[11] While it would be premature to state that Code4Lib is a truly diverse community, the adoption of a Code of Conduct for its activities and the community's sustained deliberate efforts to support inclusion are significant indicators of a permanent shift. The conference program has seen far better diversity; keynote speakers have included Valerie Aurora, Sumana Harihareswara, Kate Krauss, and Andromeda Yelton. Code4Lib and other library technology conferences, e.g. the Access Conference and the revitalized DLF Forum, are setting a new tone for library technology work.

Work in Progress—Not There Yet

Andromeda Yelton has a podcast, Open Paren, on which she interviews people who are building new structures with new tools. The ways that Yelton and her guests speak about their work with technology in and around libraries differs markedly in discursive tone and in word choice from the prevailing ways we talk about technology within IT, our libraries, and some of our conferences. One of Yelton's guests, Cecily Walker of the Vancouver Public Library, describes her work using entirely different language.[12] Speaking of her work on the quilt panel project dedicated to the murdered women from Vancouver's Downtown Eastside, she barely even mentions method or tools. Instead, she evinces a passion for the material that the project will present to the world as well as interest in the stories it tells and

---

11 "Code4lib 2008 Gender Diversity and Minority Scholarships," Code4Lib, accessed September 17, 2016, http://code4lib.org/node/208.

12 Andromeda Yelton. "Episode 1–Cecily Walker". *Open Paren*. Podcast audio, October 13, 2015, http://openparen.club/episode-1-cecily-walker. All subsequent Walker references are from this podcast.

including the voice of the community that the works represent. This was not a practiced speech nor a presentation, but rather a spontaneous conversation with a peer. Her enthusiasm for the material of the project doesn't diminish the legitimacy of her technical work on it; however, it appears that Walker employed technology as a librarian in order to complete a more traditional library project, rather than because she is a technology specialist.

Hearing Walker on Open Paren, it is easy to forget that the way she works and the reasons she does what she does are not universally found in all libraries. Typically, although not exclusively, the people with the passion for the materials and those with the technical ability to create tools are not one and the same. Many wonderfully impractical ideas coming from those who know the content wither in the atmosphere of technical vetting, mainly due to a lack of understanding and dialogue between the two camps.

Yelton's interviewees often speak directly as well as obliquely about the challenges of transgressing this divide. Walker describes how she and others in her library wanted to construct a specific type of user-friendly survey, but that doing so would require her to learn Ruby, as the IT staff had no expertise with Ruby and no capacity to learn it. Rather than giving up when faced with this obstacle—after all, it would be easy to select some other survey tool that might have been an approximation of the tool she envisioned—she opted instead to use it as motivation to learn Ruby. While it may be oversimplifying Lorde's dictum somewhat, this is a nearly literal example of seeking out new tools to build a new house, rather than persisting rigidly with the known and routine.

Progress in this direction is neither easy nor guaranteed, but rather requires effort on the part of individuals. Yelton, while speaking with Walker, addresses some of the cognitive dissonance she experiences as a programmer and a mathematician. While she does not explicitly state that she is speaking as a woman working in predominantly male spheres, intimations in this direction are clear. She noted that she doesn't "think like a programmer" and continues by noting that she did not think like a mathematician in university, either. As she framed it:

> "There's this incredibly cognitively demanding translation step from
> how I actually think about math to ways that I could admit in public

to thinking about math that wouldn't be stigmatized… How can I write it down in a way that won't fail…There are different ways to think that are legitimate."

In a subsequent podcast, Whitni Watkins, a library software developer, noted a similar fear of stigmatization, stating that she has "to reach out a lot, but it's really difficult because I think, hmm, should I, are they going to think I'm an idiot?"[13] If we stop and consider who Watkins signifies with "they" or who in Yelton's formulation will engage in stigmatizing ostensible outsiders, it is clear that the "other" they are engaging is typical programmers or mathematicians, i.e. men. These informal conversations indicate that library technical work may emphasize tools and process, expressed in particular non-inclusive ways, over and above creativity and customization of library projects. Bringing these two ways of engaging in library work together, in a person, a job description, or a unit in the library, offers us a new way of de-gendering expectations around technical competency.

In her interview with Miriam Posner, Yelton invokes the concept of "stereotype threat" and applies it to her own engagement with the library technology community, relating "I'm a lot more likely to ask for help in women-only chatrooms than in code4lib or something where I love the people but even so I still feel stereotype threat asking for help. I still feel like I can answer questions, but I shouldn't ask them."[14] Posner concurs, pointing out that on sites such as Stack Overflow that "the kind of grounds keeping and gatekeeping and disciplinary function that a lot of the commenters perform on sites like that can have a real silencing effect for a lot of people." Once we tune into these concerns, it becomes evident that it takes both courage and effort to overcome the barriers around technology communities, both within and across our organizations. These barriers are discursive and epistemological as well as physical and organizational.

---

13 Andromeda Yelton. "Episode 4–Whitni Watkins". *Open Paren*. Podcast audio, November 18, 2015, http://openparen.club/episode-4-whitni-watkins.

14 Andromeda Yelton. "Episode 3–Miriam Posner". *Open Paren*. Podcast audio, November 9, 2015, http://openparen.club/episode-3-miriam-posner. All subsequent Posner references are from this podcast.

Posner, in particular, makes clear the toll that this work takes on individuals. In reference to the Programming Historian[15], she notes that "it's not that women don't want to help," but that "they're already helping in so many other ways, all of us are, overcommitted and overtaxed and exhausted and volunteering for so many things." Yelton brings the matter to a succinct point: "It's one of the standard problems with trying to increase diversity in participation, right? All of the underrepresented people with excellent skills are already incredibly overcommitted. It's a fact." This mirrors an oft-repeated refrain one hears about increasing diversity in organizations, namely that organizations bring women or people of color into their organizations and then ask them to do not only the job they were hired to perform, but also the work of diversifying the organization.

This method does not work because it is grounded in the false notion that diversity is solved by hiring people who are different than those already in the organization. In order for libraries to become more diverse, however, they must change both the substance of their work as well as cede a share of decision-making and authority to those who represent different backgrounds and perspectives. Speaking with Yelton, Walker is unequivocal about the need to change the work:

> "There's been a lot of talk online about diversity in library and information science and it's great but all we're basically doing is trying... to fit people into a system that was not designed for them, that was basically set up for them to fail. And is that fair, or should we be looking at a way to radically redevelop the system so that it's equitable to everybody and no matter what you bring to the table. It's not a liability, it's a strength, and that can only help us be better."

We need to put the onus on organizations to change themselves, rather than expecting specific individuals to change organizations. The personal challenge an individual faces when joining an organization where their background, values, and traits are not well-represented is far from trivial, no matter how nice or well intentioned those in the dominant culture may be.

---

15 The Programming Historian publishes peer-reviewed tutorials for various digital tools that humanities scholars can use to expand their research into the realm of the digital humanities (http://programminghistorian.org/).

Beyond changing the substance of our work to include more viewpoints and ways of doing, we also need to question how we are including others in our decision-making processes. Speaking with Yelton, both Posner and Walker addressed this point explicitly, perhaps signalling how widespread the issue is as well as how difficult it is to address. Walker advocates allowing library assistants or technicians, i.e. staff without an MLS, to take on more leadership, not least because they often have decades of experience in libraries. She recognizes that "some people will say 'well that contributes to the deprofessionalization of the profession,'" but brushes such objections aside, continuing "so be it, if it means that we're getting different people into the field. I'm kind of all for that." Relating her experiences with the Programming Historian, Posner noted that she and another woman who were new to it "were relegated to the outreach section of the editorial team" but that "a) we don't just do outreach, and b) outreach is kind of a devalued field... nobody wants to be just the outreach person." This raises the critical point of how the work around technically oriented projects is valued, something she addresses by noting that it's a question of what the community respects:

> If you need to have documentation or people hanging out in the beginner chat room or whatever to have that on-ramp but then the only thing you actually respect in your community is technical contributions, then asking people to do that work, however necessary, is even more problematic.

While Posner is speaking of a voluntary community, the dynamic she describes exists in libraries as well. Academic libraries are typically rigidly hierarchical. Accordingly, work is assigned and expectations set that one must first prove one's worth and value through minor roles before being asked to take on and lead more significant projects. In order to attract as well as to retain the most talented and diverse workforce, we need to upend this practice and allow people to lead from anywhere in the organization rather than paying lip service to the idea. To repeat: we cannot build a new library with old tools.

Good intentions are not enough. We have been deliberately well intentioned for two or three decades in the form of diversity and equal opportunity statements, but haven't moved the needle much on diversity or in closing the cultural gap in our organizations. With our analysis here, we hope to have demonstrated the interrelated nature of these two issues as well as advocated for approaching the issues from an intersectional feminist perspective. This entails examining more critically the work we do within our organizations, deliberately changing our work to include voices and viewpoints that truly reflect the communities we serve, communicating this new focus to potential hires to encourage them to join the organization, and granting them the ability and authority to shape their work and direction.

Bibliography

Beinecke Rare Book & Manuscript Library. "Collection Highlights." Accessed April 13, 2016. http://beinecke.library.yale.edu/collections/highlights.

Chun, Wendy Hui Kyong. *Programmed Visions: Software and Memory.* Cambridge: MIT Press, 2014.

Code4lib. "2008 Gender Diversity and Minority Scholarships." *code4lib*, December 17, 2007. https://code4lib.org/node/208.

Lorde, Audre. *Sister Outsider: Essays and Speeches.* Crossing Press Feminist Series. Trumansburg, NY: Crossing Press, 1984.

Sadler, Bess, and Chris Bourg. "Feminism and the Future of Library Discovery." *The Code4Lib Journal*, no. 28 (April 15, 2015). http://journal.code4lib.org/articles/10425.

Schonfeld, Roger. "Organizing the Work of the Research Library." Ithaka S+R, August 18, 2016. doi: 10.18665/sr.283717.

Shirazi, Roxanne. "Reproducing the Academy: Librarians and the Question of Service in the Digital Humanities." *Roxanne Shirazi*, July 15, 2014. https://roxanneshirazi.com/2014/07/15/reproducing-the-academy-librarians-and-the-question-of-service-in-the-digital-humanities/.

Yelton, Andromeda. "Episode 1–Cecily Walker". *Open Paren*. Podcast audio, October 13, 2015. http://openparen.club/episode-1-cecily-walker.

————. "Episode 3–Miriam Posner". *Open Paren*. November 9, 2015. http://openparen.club/episode-3-miriam-posner.

————. "Episode 4–Whitni Watkins". *Open Paren*. November 18, 2015. http://openparen.club/episode-4-whitni-watkins.

Feminist Praxis in Library Leadership

April M. Hathcock and Jennifer Vinopal

Introduction

We all agree feminist leadership is a good thing, but what does it even mean? What makes leadership feminist? These questions, innocently posed over a friendly discussion, led to more questions and more discussions, which served as the foundation for this research and book chapter. As friends who frequently delve into discussions of race, whiteness, feminism, intersectionality, and the library profession, we realized that this opening question was more than a rhetorical conversation starter: We wanted answers. And when we looked to existing library literature and found little in the way of response, we realized that there existed a research gap that we could fill.

For both of us, this research project has grown out of our own personal scholarship. April has been doing extensive work examining intersections of identity, oppressive normativity, whiteness, and the ways these concepts play out in the library profession.[1] Jennifer's work critically examines diversity and inclusion practices, intersectional feminist praxis, and whiteness

---

1 April Hathcock, "White Librarianship in Blackface: Diversity Initiatives in LIS," *In the Library With the Lead Pipe* (October 7, 2015), http://www.inthelibrarywiththeleadpipe. org/2015/lis-diversity/; and April Hathcock, *At the Intersection* (blog), https:// aprilhathcock.wordpress.com/.

in the information profession.[2] As a result of her work in this area, Jennifer was asked to serve as the closing keynote speaker for the 2015 Taiga Forum in Vancouver, British Columbia, during which she proposed a birds of a feather discussion on feminist leadership. At the end of a long and thought-provoking discussion, Shirley Lew, one of the editors of this volume, asked a crucial question that hits on the very essence of our research: "Isn't feminist leadership just about being a decent human being?"

In this research study, we take this simple yet provocative question as a starting point for an exploration of how feminist theories inform the thinking and practice of library leaders. How can feminism, in particular intersectional feminism, help us think critically about core library values such as diversity, inclusivity, and respect? How does a feminist praxis affect organizational culture? Can feminism help us become better mentors for the next generation of leaders? Could we better address the diversity problem in the profession? How is feminist-informed leadership different from just being "a decent human being"? And what does this all look like in practice?

We decided to ask feminist leaders in the library profession how their feminist values inform and affect everyday management and leadership activities such as staffing, mentoring, policy development, and decision-making. In this way, we hoped to provide readers with real-life examples of the everyday practice of feminism in library leadership, to offer practical approaches that others can adopt or adapt, and to understand some of the challenges in bringing an overt feminist praxis into our library practice.

It is important to note how knowledge and meaning are created in this chapter. We recognize that what our interview subjects shared with us was constructed through their own experiences, shaped by their memories, and then further molded through their selection of which experiences to recount to us and how. As interviewers, we brought our own experiences, knowledge, biases, and agendas to the interviews that we conducted and to how we interpreted and recorded the meaning of our interviewees' words. The technology we used to conduct the interviews, the interview method, the timing we

---

2 Jennifer Vinopal, "The Quest for Diversity in Library Staffing: From Awareness to Action," *In the Library With the Lead Pipe* (January 13, 2016), http://www.inthelibrarywiththeleadpipe.org/2016/quest-for-diversity/; and Jennifer Vinopal, *Library Sphere* (blog), http://vinopal.org/blog/.

imposed on our conversations, all served to shape and construct the information that we now analyze and present here.

Our experiences and biases also manifest as we write, as we choose what to emphasize and what to exclude, what meaning we make of it, and the words we use to express ourselves. DeVault and Gross, in their article on feminist interviewing, recommend:

> An awareness that researchers are always working with accounts constructed linguistically, that experience recounted is always emergent in the moment, that telling requires a listener and that the listening shapes the account as well as the telling, that both telling and listening are shaped by discursive histories (so that fragments of many other tellings are carried in any embodied conversation), and so on.[3]

Thus, we approach this work with that awareness, knowing that as a straight cisgender white woman from the United States Northeast and a straight cisgender black woman from the U.S. South, we bring our own experiences, backgrounds, histories, and preconceived ideas to bear, even as we look to our research participants to make meaning in our work. For us, this is a deeply personal work to fill a much-needed gap in the library literature on feminist leadership praxis.

REVIEW OF THE LITERATURE

Jean Lau Chin notes in the abstract of her 2003 Presidential Address before the Division 35 Society for the Psychology of Women, "[a]lthough the theories and models on feminism and leadership exist, there has been little study of the intersection of the two."[4] Fourteen years later, at the publication of this current volume, Chin's observation still holds true, particularly in the realm of library and information studies. Much of the literature we reviewed for this study either focused on gendered differences in leadership styles and outcomes in LIS or focused on the application of feminist theory to the practice of library and information studies work, without a particular view toward the practice of leadership.

3 Marjorie L. DeVault and Glenda Gross, "Feminist Interviewing: Experience, Talk, and Knowledge," in *Handbook of Feminist Research: Theory and Praxis*, ed. Sharlene Nagy Hesse-Biber (Thousand Oaks, CA: SAGE, 2007), 179.

4 Jean Lau Chin, "2003 Division 35 Presidential Address: Feminist Leadership: Feminist Visions and Diverse Voices," *Psychology of Women Quarterly* 28 (2004): 1.

With regards to gendered differences in leadership development and expectations in library and information professions, we made particular note of two articles, one from the mid-1980s and one from 2015. In her 1985 survey of male and female public library directors in the U.S., Joy Greiner uncovers significant differences based on gender in career development options, support, salary, and resources.[5] Likewise, two decades later, in their piece on gendered expectations of library leaders, Jessica Olin and Michelle Millet find similar trends at play, including gendered differences in the ways library leaders are treated by their staff and colleagues.[6] In addition, Olin and Millet call for an end to the binary method of examining gender in library leadership, with a view toward building a more gender-inclusive examination of library leadership issues.

While these studies and others like them have been important in uncovering the gendered issues that arise in library and information studies leadership, they do not examine the role that feminist theory and practice can play in the development and day-to-day work of library leaders. On the other hand, there has been an increasing amount of research surfacing in the library literature regarding the application of feminist theory to library practice apart from leadership. In their piece on feminist theory and library discovery, Bess Sadler and Chris Bourg reject the myth of library neutrality and expose the ways in which a feminist approach can guide library interactions centered on advocacy and embodiment.[7] Likewise, in her book about feminist pedagogy in library instruction, Maria Accardi examines the way that feminist theory can be applied to library instruction to enhance librarian-student relationships and promote an enriched and embodied learning experience.[8]

---

5 Joy Greiner, "A Comparative Study of the Career Development Patterns of Male and Female Library Administrators in Large Public Libraries," *Library Trends* 34, no. 2 (1985): 280-81.

6 Jessica Olin and Michelle Millet, "Gendered Expectations for Leadership in Libraries," *In the Library With the Lead Pipe* (November 4, 2015), http://www.inthelibrarywiththeleadpipe.org/2015/libleadgender/.

7 Bess Sadler and Chris Bourg, "Feminism and The Future of Library Discovery," *Code4Lib Journal*, no. 28 (April 15, 2015), http://journal.code4lib.org/articles/10425.

8 Maria T. Accardi, ed., *Feminist Pedagogy for Library Instruction* (Sacramento: Library Juice Press, 2013).

As with the studies on gendered differences in library leadership opportunities, this work on the application of feminist theory to general library practice is key for the profession, but it does not capture the ways in which feminist theory can apply to library leadership specifically. In fact, the only study in the library literature that discusses the link between feminism and library leadership is a 2014 study by Marta Deyrup. In her work, Deyrup surveyed over 200 women library administrators for their opinions on second-wave feminism and the ways it has affected their career opportunities in library leadership.[9] While the study combines an examination of leadership and feminist theory, it does so within the context of gendered differences in the perception of and opportunities for library leadership and not within the context of applying feminist practice to the work of library leadership. Further, Deyrup's study focuses entirely on female library leaders and in many ways conflates *feminine* leadership traits with *feminist* leadership traits. The former focuses on the ways in which women lead differently from men, while the latter focuses on applying the theory and praxis of feminism to one's leadership work, regardless of gender identity. A focus on feminine leadership traits runs the risk of being essentialist in its approach and analysis and is not as helpful to understanding the ways that feminist theory, and its attendant concerns with social justice, can be activated in library leadership practice by all leaders, regardless of their gender identity.

Given the lack of research available specifically on feminist leadership in the library literature, we broadened our scope to look at existing feminist leadership research in education, a related field. We enlarged our scope even further to encompass research in secondary as well as higher education, in which we both work. We also looked at research beyond North America, where we both are based, to work that is being done in other parts of the world.

As a theoretical basis for our research, we relied heavily on Jill Blackmore's work on applying feminist theory to teacher and

---

9 Marta Deyrup, "Academic Library Leadership, Second-Wave Feminism, and Twenty-First Century Humanism: Reflections on a Changing Profession," in *Leadership in Academic Libraries Today: Connecting Theory to Practice*, eds. Bradford Lee Eden and Jody Condit Fagan (Lanham, MD: Rowman & Littlefield, 2014), 91-107.

administrator leadership in Australian secondary schools.[10] Blackmore takes a systemic approach to examining the role of feminist leadership in promoting a more just and equitable educational system for students, parents, and teachers. She examines the power dynamics within the Australian school system in general and within certain schools in particular. Her goal is to apply feminist theory in such a way as to "orient leadership in the educational setting toward social justice within an intersectional context."[11] As she notes, "For feminists, leadership is about gendered power relations that impact on social justice. . . . Focusing on social justice mean[s] . . . addressing issues of inequality, power, responsibility and ethics."[12] To this end, Blackmore views feminist leadership as being a phenomenon that can occur at any level of the educational institution and is not limited to administrator-level responsibilities.[13] In addition, she is cautious throughout her work to distinguish between the application of *feminist* leadership theory for social justice and *feminine* leadership theory, which results in an essentialist view of leadership rooted in gender binaries.[14]

In terms of methodology, we looked to the work of Jane Strachan and Tracy Barton to examine ways of applying feminist research methodology to the research of feminist leadership in education. In her study of three secondary school principals in New Zealand, all of whom self-identified as feminists, Strachan adopted a feminist research methodology to study the ways in which feminist leadership, rooted in emancipatory politics, informed the day-to-day work of school administrators.[15] Employing a feminist qualitative research design, Strachan conducted a series of semi-structured interviews with the study participants, as well as observing them first hand at work and reviewing documents relevant to their work. Though all three

10 Jill Blackmore, *Troubling Women: Feminism, Leadership, and Educational Change* (Buckingham: Open University Press, 1999), 1-20; and Jill Blackmore, "Social Justice and the Study and Practice of Leadership in Education: A Feminist History," *Journal of Educational Administration and History* 38, no. 2 (2006): 185-200.

11 Blackmore, "Social Justice," 187.

12 Ibid.

13 Blackmore, *Troubling Women*, 6.

14 Ibid., 18.

15 Jane Strachan, "Feminist Educational Leadership: Locating the Concepts in Practice," *Gender and Education* 11, no. 3 (1999): 309-22.

participants were women, in her analysis Strachan is cautious to avoid characterizing feminine leadership rather than feminist leadership: "Essentialism masks the differences in feminist leadership philosophy and practice and can be destructive in that it hides much of the rich tapestry of how leadership is practised by different feminists working in different contexts."[16] Instead, she takes an intersectional approach to her work, noting the ways that race, culture, class, geography, as well as gender, affect the work of the women—two white and one Pacific Islander—she interviewed. Strachan concludes that these women engage in active, creative, and flexible feminist practice to build caring educational communities that best serve the needs of their students and the students' families.

Using a similar feminist methodology, Tracy Barton, relying in part on Strachan's previous work, conducted a study of feminist leadership among seven women higher education administrators in the Midwestern U.S.[17] Barton engaged in semi-structured interviews with the participants who self-identified as feminists and who represented a variety of institutional, professional, and racial/ethnic backgrounds. In her analysis, Barton takes an intersectional approach to her findings, drawing out a number of emergent themes and relating them back to the ways in which they interact with the interviewees' varying racial, ethnic, sexual, and even religious identities. Some of the more common themes Barton uncovers in her study include fairness, equity, and justice; voice; marginalization; and community development.[18] For all of the women, these themes play key roles in their feminist leadership practice, a finding that bears out in our own examination within the library context.

Methodology

As feminists talking to other feminists in order to write a chapter about how feminism informs leadership practice, it was a natural

---

16 Strachan, "Feminist Educational Leadership," 311.

17 Tracy R. Barton, "A Feminist Construction of Leadership in American Higher Education" (Ph.D. diss., University of Toledo, 2006), ProQuest (UMI 3264478); and Tracy R. Barton, "Feminist Leadership: Building Nurturing Academic Communities," *Advancing Women in Leadership* 22 (2006).

18 Barton, "A Feminist Construction," 172-77; and Barton, "Feminist Leadership," n.p.

choice for us to choose a feminist research method for our study. In light of the methods used in Strachan's and Barton's works, we decided to conduct in-depth personal interviews using a general interview guide approach in order, literally, to *give voice* to feminist library leaders on this little-studied topic. While no research methods are inherently feminist in their own right, qualitative methods that elicit new knowledge on feminist practice and also provide a means to interrogate the research process itself are particularly valued by feminists.[19] In keeping with our feminist approach, we designed a set of open-ended questions that would guide our conversation with each of the interviewees, while still keeping the topic open enough for participants to shape the discussions as we went.

In order to identify interviewees, we mined our professional networks, looking for colleagues whose words or actions within a public context indicated a feminist perspective, for example, speaking or publishing on topics relevant to intersectional feminism, critical librarianship, or queer or critical race theory. In addition to a feminist perspective, we looked for participants who evinced functional leadership within the profession, which might be demonstrated through, for example, their influence on the shape and direction of professional conversations and thought, a commitment to developing new leaders, an impact on platforms or tools (technical or analog) that promote an open or social justice agenda, or ongoing work to influence policy at a national or international level. For us, the distinction between functional (or situational) leadership and positional (or by-appointment) leadership is crucial: While not mutually exclusive, we do not assume that everyone appointed to high-level positions in the profession are necessarily performing leadership as we define it. Instead, we focused on those feminists who exert influence on our profession, no matter their place within the professional hierarchy or their longevity within librarianship.

Our eleven participants, to whom we have promised anonymity so they would feel free to say things they might not otherwise have shared, represent a diverse set of perspectives and identities. We included people of different ages, gender identities and expressions,

---

19 Sharon Brisolara, "Feminist Theory: Its Domains and Applications," in *Feminist Evaluation and Research: Theory and Practice*, eds. Sharon Brisolara, Denise Seigart, and Saumitra SenGupta (New York: The Guildford Press, 2014), 19.

sexual orientations, abilities, races, and ethnicities, and we sought representation from different-sized organizations, both public and private. Six of our interviewees were people of color, and five were white. Three use gender pronouns he/him/his, seven use gender pronouns she/her/hers, and one uses the gender pronouns they/them/theirs. Three are early career professionals, three mid-career, and five have more seniority in the profession. Seven currently live and work on the East Coast of the United States, two on the West Coast of the United States, and two in Western Canada.

The selection criteria and our method for identifying interviewees are subjective and prone to bias. Because we relied on our own professional networks to identify participants, of the initial list of more than thirty potential interviewees, all were personally known to at least one of us. Since we had limited time for interviews, and in order to ensure diversity in our final set, we narrowed the list to eleven based on our knowledge of the participants and the various experiences and perspectives we thought they would bring to our conversations and our thinking on the topic. Given more time, we might have used a snowball sampling method (also prone to bias) in order to enlarge our set.[20]

No matter how collaborative and open-ended we were in our conversations with participants, we acknowledge the imbalance of power in a setting where we, the authors, would ultimately get to assign meaning to the data collected. In her chapter "Feminist Theory: Its Domains and Applications," Brisolara presents six key feminist principles of evaluation that all have bearing on our own methodology:

- Knowledge is culturally, socially, and temporally contingent.

- Knowledge is a powerful resource that serves an explicit or implicit purpose.

- Evaluation is a political activity; evaluators' personal experiences, perspectives, and characteristics come from and lead to a particular political stance.

---

20 Snowball sampling involves asking initial research participants to suggest additional participants, allowing the sample to increase or "snowball." Kathi N. Miner, Toby Epstein Jayaratne, Amanda Pesonen, and Lauren Zurbrügg. "Using Survey Research as a Quantitative Method for Feminist Social Change." In *Handbook of Feminist Research: Theory and Praxis*, by Sharlene Nagy Hesse-Biber (Thousand Oaks, CA: SAGE, 2007), 210.

- Research methods, institutions, and practices are social constructs.

- There are multiple ways of knowing.

- Gender inequities are one manifestation of social injustice. Discrimination cuts across race, class, and culture and is inextricably linked to all three.[21]

We, therefore, make no claims to objectivity in this study. Rather, our purpose was to mine the experiences of a small set of feminist leaders in order to *collaboratively* make meaning of the research topic through open-ended, guided conversation. We believe that this subjective and subject-oriented method is, indeed, complementary to our openly political agenda, which is to promote research on and use of feminist leadership practices in libraries.

TECHNICAL CONSIDERATIONS

After confirming that this study was exempted by our local institutional review board from full review, we contacted our potential interviewees, inviting them to participate in our research, and all eleven readily agreed. We told them the general topics we would discuss, how the interview would be structured, and that we would record the interviews only to help us in our note taking and analysis. We assured them that we would not publish the recordings and would destroy them at the end of the project.

For the interviews, we formulated open-ended interview questions to elicit responses on the following topics:

- What is feminism?

- What is leadership?

- What are some examples of your feminist leadership actions?

- How are you addressing issues of diversity and inclusion?

- What do you read that informs your feminism and/or your leadership?

- What other related topics would you like to tell us about?

---

21 Brisolara, "Feminist Theory," 23-29.

During the interviews, we took turns reading interview questions and gave each other space to probe and pursue topics as they came up. We conducted the interviews with Skype and recorded audio with QuickTime. We then used an auto-captioning tool provided by our institution as a first pass to create transcriptions and cleaned them manually. Once we had accurate transcripts, we clustered the interviewees' quotes thematically by creating a document listing the key topics discussed in the interviews and then copying quotes from the transcripts into the relevant theme areas within the document. As we discovered other recurring topics that interviewees discussed, we added them to the document along with the relevant quotes.

COMMON THEMES

We were overwhelmed by the wealth of knowledge, experience, and personal stories participants were willing to share with us. In analyzing the data, we uncovered three broad themes, corresponding to general questions from our interviews:

- What does being a feminist mean to you?

- What makes leadership feminist?

- What tips or advice do you have for others looking to activate their feminism at work?

What Does Being a Feminist Mean to You?

One of the first questions we asked each of our interviewees was, "What does being a feminist mean to you?" While we approached this research with our own preconceived ideas about what constituted a feminist and had even selected our research participants based on those ideas, we wanted to begin our interviews by laying those preconceived notions aside in order to hear from our participants, in their own voices, what it meant to engage in feminist praxis.

Interestingly, one common thread that surfaced in many of their responses was the fact that their personal definitions of feminism were rooted more in their embodied experiences than in any sort of textbook understanding of feminist theory:

> I was thinking just what would my definition be and I think I don't
> know that I could actually come up with one and I really struggled
> because it's always been such a part of my life.
>
> I think I would probably say that I have had an inclination and
> an orientation toward women's issues, towards feminist issues and
> issues of race and class in my work and in my professional practice
> for a long time. But really became much more conscious when . .
> . [describes hearing someone at a conference describe interviewee's
> work as "feminist"] . . .So there was that moment of crystallisation
> where I was listening to somebody else describing my work, thinking
> "Oh yeah, right, you put all that together and, you know, that's a
> feminist!"
>
> There was a roundtable informal discussion that sprung up as a part
> of the work we were doing. To be honest, in public that might have
> been the first time that I ever decided to identify as a feminist. It was
> crazy hard. It was something I had never done before. It's not to say
> in any way that I haven't thought about it and in some ways try to
> practice some of the principles there. But that was sort of my first
> coming out, if you will.

For many of our participants, feminist praxis was a part of their lives
and politics, long before they knew or thought to use the label.

In some ways, this natural link between embodied experience and
feminism may have arisen from a connection between realization of
feminist identity and interaction with others. As the last two quotes
above demonstrate, several of our participants came into their self-
identity as feminists from their interactions with other feminists.
For at least one of our participants, this interaction began early in
childhood through a relationship with a feminist parent:

> I guess for me in order to answer that question I have to go back
> to my childhood. The fact that I was raised by a feminist. And my
> mother was a big influence on me. . . . So I just had a very heightened
> sense of feminism as an active, real-life thing that had consequences
> for people in my whole family, I guess you might say.

Despite this connection between interpersonal relationships, embodied
experience, and feminist self-identity, however, participants expressed
discomfort recognizing having any sort of expertise or authority in
the realm of feminist theory. Repeatedly participants lamented that
they did not know enough feminist theory or had not read enough

feminist theorists to be able to give an authoritative perspective on what it means to be a feminist:

> But that's definitely an area that I feel like I sometimes get impostor syndrome, like, "Oh, I don't know enough" or "I need to read more" or "Let me pull up a Wikipedia article." . . . However, I feel like I need to read more all the time.

> I haven't read enough about intersectional feminism as a theory to be, like, that's my home.

> And so I think that's why I'm more and more aware lately that I'm behind in my reading and I need to catch up.

> I don't always feel like I'm totally well-read in it. In theory per se.

Moreover, several participants asked, at the end of the interview, that we share our personal reading lists with them so that they could "catch up" on their feminist reading. We gladly complied with these requests while assuring all our participants of how much they had to teach us and others about being a feminist leader. Their feelings of inadequacy notwithstanding, interview participants described the kinds of critical work that influences them: queer theory, critical race theory, intersectional feminist theory, critical pedagogy and librarianship. They specifically named Michel Foucault, Sara Ahmed, bell hooks (*Teaching to Transgress*), Roxanne Gay (*Bad Feminist*), Kimberlé Crenshaw, Patricia Hill-Collins (*Black Feminist Thought*), Adrienne Rich (*Of Woman Born*), and Rebecca Traister (*All the Single Ladies*),[22] who have given them insight into the power politics of the workplace, intersectional oppression, and, as one of our interviewees said, the "gendered aspects of everyday life" in the library profession.

In terms of applying an intersectional context to their feminism, all participants identified their feminism as being necessarily intersectional. For them, feminism could not meaningfully exist without considerations of other axes of oppression, such as race, sexual orientation, class, disability, and other marginalized identities:

> I would say that it always comes down to fighting for and advocating for gender equality. And that's also taking into account the ideas of intersectionality. So for me feminism should encompass all women

---

22 Here we include specific book titles if interviewees mentioned them.

and all women's experiences, not just necessarily what has historically been the interests of white feminism.

Being a feminist means to me that I think about power dynamics in the workplace, but [also] in interpersonal relationships. That I have an awareness, that I'm bringing to my own and to others' awareness power dynamics within institutions and interpersonal relationships. So that can be about gender; it can be about the dynamics between women and men. But for me it very much also means on other axes of power, so around race, class, ability, any kind of things where power dynamics get skewed and where, particularly in a work setting, particularly where the institution plays a role and imbalances get systematized. That's what I think feminism is.

You know, I have a broad-based commitment to justice and equality so I think when a lot of people think about feminism, it's just situated in equality for women. And I think the larger, over time, the bigger picture way that I've thought about it is really in terms of intersectionality. So it's not just addressing the fact that people are unequal; it's really beginning to examine the structure of those systems and how they interplay. How racism is reflected in the systems we build as well as the economic structures that are formed out of these systems.

For me, patriarchy is intimately bound with white supremacy and heterosexism. They're part of the package. . . . But I would say, interestingly, being involved in the library community has deepened my understanding of feminism, or broadened it, whatever the word is, particularly in respect to intersectionality.

Yeah, I think it's hard to talk about that without talking about race, too. Especially since I'm sure you know black feminism is different sometimes than white feminism. So you're advocating for both, for people of color and for women, too.

A few of our participants actually identified more readily with another axis of identity and oppression, that is, sexual orientation, and placed that identity at the fore of their feminist work:

It's interesting because I think of myself as a queer before I think of myself as a feminist. But I guess, you know, feminism means equity and fair distribution of opportunities and life chances. And I believe in that and I believe in that for all people. And not just for women. . . . I would love a feminism that was big enough that I didn't feel like I had to qualify it. Yeah, a hundred percent. Right, like that everybody is constructed based on different kinds of systems and have different kinds of identities related to those systems. I haven't read enough about intersectional feminism as a theory to be, like that's my home. But I definitely believe that women have multiple identities. You know, no one boils down to a single identity.

I see these intersections and again I identify as a gay [person of color] and I feel like there are all these kind of things that overlap and intersect. So seeing myself represented or not being represented . . . that there is this kind of template that you can also overlay when it comes to what it means to be a feminist, you know being a woman in this profession. You know these things overlap and they intersect and they mirror each other. . . . I look at, say, what it is to be a [non-white] librarian also applies to being a gay librarian, also applies to being a feminist librarian. In this, you know, crazy mixed up world of librarianship.

For all participants, being a feminist involved embodied knowledge and experience, firmly rooted in intersectionality and the multiple ways that identity and power interplay.

What Makes Leadership Feminist?

Ironically, despite everyone's willingness, even excitement, to talk to us about the topic, most interviewees expressed some doubts about the possibility of feminist leadership. In some this manifested as surprise that we considered them leaders in the profession at all. Other interviewees were ambivalent about the tension between the ideals and values of feminism, as they define it, and the idea of leadership from the top levels of an organization, because of the potential for power imbalance and the fear that this power might compromise one's values.

Despite these concerns, interviewees saw feminism as an antidote to power-wielding, ego-driven leadership, and saw it as providing a set of values and practices akin to the kind of "practice of freedom" in education that bell hooks advocates.[23] They all felt that feminist leadership is not the same as other kinds of leadership; it's definitely not positional. For many, feminist leadership is about moving people toward a common goal through influence (not ego), and one of the crucial roles of a leader is to look for and develop people within the organization, wherever they are in rank, who have the potential to

23 bell hooks, *Teaching to Transgress* (New York: Routledge, 1994), 4. hooks emphasizes "the difference between education as the practice of freedom and education that merely strives to reinforce domination."

become leaders and affect positive organizational change in their own right. This is especially true if they don't "fit the mold" of a typical library leader.

Thus, when asked to describe what specifically makes leadership feminist, as opposed to more traditional, non-feminist forms of leadership, participants focused on the importance of employing leadership styles and methods in the service of feminist values, such as community building, creating a safe environment, valuing diversity, empowering others, and information sharing. For all of our participants, feminist leadership centers on acknowledging sources of power and leveraging that power for the benefit of those working for and with them in the organization:

> I think that first and foremost the responsibility of a leader is to the people that he or she is charged to serve.

> With intersectional feminist leadership, one of the things that you're really looking at is making sure that you're not just advancing the company, but you're advancing and progressing people. That you're not just meeting a business or an organizational bottom line, you're actually committed to the idea of helping people become empowered so that they can change their lives and they can change their communities.

> As feminists we always keep in mind the equality aspect; that's one of the biggest things. As a feminist you're always thinking of equality and retention anyways. So you're always thinking "How can I make this better for this person? How can I help keep this person?" It's always in the back of your mind. They are really hand-in-hand.

Feminist leadership is ultimately about correcting for power imbalances and doing so in an open, intentional, and purposeful way. For our interviewees, there is no room for neutrality in feminist leadership:

> I think feminist leadership is explicitly political; it explicitly acknowledges the role of power. It explicitly understands that if I do A, I can't do B. And there are implications for why I'm doing that.

> Sharing power I see as pretty significant in terms of what I value in leadership or what I see in leadership.

> Feminist leadership would be about sharing power, redistributing powers. Making sure that everyone has opportunities. I've never lost anything when someone else got something good.

Our participants see their feminist leadership as a means of enacting feminist ideals in their organizations and within the profession to the benefit of all.

In the quest to achieve these feminist ideals, interviewees, especially those higher up in their organization's hierarchy, see information sharing as a feminist act and as a way to redistribute power and undermine those intransigent structures:

> I'm aware that knowledge is power, and that as much knowledge as I can share with my organization, you know, that's a way of sharing power. And there's a bit of a culture of keeping things, of not sharing. So wherever I can, unless there's reasons for personnel or sensitive budget decisions or something like that, I share information.
>
> I am absolutely transparent about everything that I do. I am an over-communicator and I think that's a big part of my feminist ethic at work. It's like everybody knows everything as I know it.

Others specifically highlighted the need for transparency around decision-making processes. Moreover, as they share knowledge and power, they also give others voice in an environment where they might otherwise not be heard. One participant noted,

> There are certain people who are very comfortable when an issue is thrown on the table, like they'll always be able to speak, and they'll voice their opinion and they'll speak more than once and they'll take up lots of space. And so we always hear from them. But there are other really smart folks around the table who aren't comfortable in that kind of a setting.

These feminist leaders use their power, their political acumen, and self-knowledge to build supportive communities and workplaces, to think critically about whose voices are centered and whose are marginalized in our profession, and to expose and rectify the inequitable power dynamics in the systems that surround us.

What Tips or Advice Do You have For Others Looking to Activate Their Feminism at Work?

As our goal in conducting this research is to reveal the everyday practice of feminism in library leadership, we asked interviewees to tell us about practical approaches that others can adopt or adapt. They also shared some of the challenges in bringing an overt feminist praxis into their library work. Overall, participants insisted on the primacy of praxis in their feminism. In a nutshell, if you're just thinking, reading, and theorizing, but you're not doing, you're not doing it right. As one colleague offered, "Theory does have its place as long as there's also action that can come out of that, too." Yet they also emphasized that theory provides a critical perspective for analyzing and strategizing about the day to day. One said, "My approach to leadership becomes more holistic over time the more I read, the more I learn." The practices they discussed reflect the five key feminist values mentioned above—community building, creating a safe environment, valuing diversity, empowering others, and information sharing—which themselves require the ability to understand one's own relationship to power, and a willingness to use it to benefit others. They said:

> Be honest about what kind of power you have.
>
> Self reflection and knowing yourself is one of the most important things that you can do.
>
> Be prepared to do the work.

As a precondition to "doing the work," the first and most important thing all participants urged is developing a community or network to rely on:

> Find your people and make use of your people and work your network.
>
> That's going to be important because there will be people who will oppose you, and will provide many, many opportunities for you to be blocked.
>
> You can feel a little crazy and a reality check from people who you trust and who are like-minded is super helpful.

Participants also recommended not relying solely on your immediate colleagues for support:

> Throw out the org chart when you're looking for allies.
>
> Make connections across the entire system.
>
> Those networks need to be outside of your institution.
>
> If you hear somebody speak at a conference or write a blog post or something that inspires you or that you relate to, talk to them.

In particular, social media was singled out by many as a particularly helpful place to find support.

Participants also talked about creating safe, inclusive environments in which to promote feminist values. As one participant explained,

> It's really about creating this framework. It's about signaling that the organization is a place [where] that kind of conversation can happen and that action can happen.

These leaders take responsibility for the welfare of others:

> My first responsibility is to everyone that works here at the library and to make sure that I'm doing everything I can to look out for their well-being and their professional development. That's first and foremost.

Along these lines, participants discussed how important it is to interrupt harmful behavior, which they strive to do effectively and respectfully. Whether to confront someone publicly or privately depends on the situation, but overall, such correction is meant to interrupt in the instant as well as to teach:

> If I see an injustice, if I see ugliness, I'm going to say something.

> If I'm there I intervene immediately. I don't try to do it in an aggressive manner because I don't believe in upbraiding people in . . . public. I don't believe in humiliating people.

> So I have actually been pretty stern with a couple of...young men [exhibiting harmful behaviour] in private conversation but in a way that didn't humiliate them in front of a group [and] I think has helped them actually take it to heart.

Participants noted that confronting harmful behavior can be a community effort:

> My impulse is not to be directly confrontational but to have other people collectively operate against that force in that instance.

Nonetheless, confrontation is difficult:

> There are some cases where the best and most appropriate thing is to pull somebody aside and have a private conversation. . . . And then there are other times where I wonder if that approach . . . [is] actually kind of an act of cowardice on my part.

> We want to be nice and we want everyone to like us and the repercussions can be ugly.

One participant, however, acknowledged, "social media is a whole different thing. You know on social media I'll just call people straight out." Finally, when building safe and inclusive spaces, participants recognized the importance of self-care, which may include disengaging from a toxic space or conversation when it becomes too time consuming, detrimental, or simply pointless. As one summed up, "There's no way that you can inspire other people if you're so burnt out yourself."

In addition to cultivating safe spaces, these leaders spend a significant amount of time empowering others and providing them opportunities to grow through advocacy, policy setting, and mentoring: "Making opportunities for other people is important." Participants actively seek out occasions to cultivate leadership in others, especially those who might otherwise be overlooked as potential leaders. One explained,

> How I put this into action is in actively thinking about opportunity for leadership and for development of people in my institution and of people in the profession who may not put themselves forward or nominate themselves for a role, but I know they would be fantastic. If they were a member of a more privileged group or if they had had different opportunities, maybe they would be putting themselves forward but they don't. I will actively try to tap those people, encourage them, support them, and offer the kind of mentorship either by myself or through someone else, to allow them to succeed and to help them to develop.

Cultivating leaders is also a matter of timing. Regarding a colleague who is a working parent, a participant explained,

> This is a matter of people having the balance in their life that they want. You know, in five years her kids are not going to be in daycare anymore and she's still going to have all the skills and abilities that she's got now. . . . I talk explicitly and support parents in the workplace. For me that is about developing women leaders.

Other day-to-day ways to "make opportunities for other people" include publicly giving credit, structuring meetings in ways that value different communication styles, modeling the behavior you want to cultivate in the organization, and openly acknowledging the power you have and the values that underlie your work.

Regarding the overwhelming and persistent homogeneity of the library profession,[24] participants strive to build diverse and inclusive workplaces through hiring, promotion, and the personal and personnel work needed to create inclusive spaces. Many mentioned the under-representation of staff in the profession based on race and ethnicity, and the additional gender disparities in technology fields. Participants also noted disparities in terms of rank:

> The group that was left out and being marginalized in [my] organization were the support staff and I know that's a tension in a lot of libraries.

In supporting career and leadership development among people from underrepresented groups, participants talked about ensuring that early career librarians of color have time and opportunities to gain the skills and experiences to make them successful. Using words like "maneuvering" and "negotiation," some described strategies for influencing the hiring process in order to increase the likelihood of hiring underrepresented candidates, calling this invisible but important work. In describing candidate evaluation processes, participants related common strategies:

> When I am faced with a choice between two candidates…I'm looking at a candidate as, not only are they qualified (because if they weren't qualified on paper they never would have made it through the door), but where I can do some redress to give them additional points on their answers. And sometimes it works. And sometimes it doesn't.

> I generally try to couch it in those things that are quantitative rather than qualitative. So even though I might be making my assessment based on qualitative criteria, [I'm] trying to describe it in a quantitative way.

> I might say something like 'Why are we always picking the same kinds of people?'

---

24 Chris Bourg, "The Unbearable Whiteness of Librarianship," *Feral Librarian* (blog), March 3, 2014, https://chrisbourg.wordpress.com/2014/03/03/the-unbearable-whiteness-of-librarianship/; and Angela Galvan, "Soliciting Performance, Hiding Bias: Whiteness and Librarianship," *In the Library With the Lead Pipe* (June 3, 2015), http://www.inthelibrarywiththeleadpipe.org/2015/soliciting-performance-hiding-bias-whiteness-and-librarianship/.

Nevertheless, this work is hard and the challenges may seem intractable:

> I am sick of talking about diversity and inclusion. . . . If I don't do this work, no one else is going to do this work. It's exhausting in the age of Trayvon Martin. It's exhausting in the age of Eric Garner. . . . It's exhausting that in 2016 librarianship looks the way that it does. . . . And I really would love to just talk about how students learn. . . . But you know I look around our office and no one else is gonna do it.

> We're spending all our time trying to prepare [underrepresented people] to succeed in our profession. How about if we prepare ourselves to create inclusive workplaces? Do we know how to do that?

These participants are struggling daily to realize the feminist ideals of "equality and empowerment and equal access," using their power against the intransigent "structures which seem incredibly unwieldy and totally out of our control."

CONCLUSION

The common thread that weaves through all of our participants' remarks on intersectional feminist leadership in the library profession is the ability to acknowledge one's own power and use it to advance explicitly feminist values that benefit others. To claim one's power and influence is not necessarily easy; it requires self-knowledge and honesty about where that power originates, be it from organizational position, or the privileges of race, gender, class, or any other demographic criteria overvalued in our culture. As one participant acknowledged, "Maybe I need to do more work to own the power that I do have to shape what happens at my organization." You can't share your power unless you accept that you have it in the first place.

This study intended to demonstrate what feminist leadership looks like in the library profession, but it barely scratches the surface. More critical work remains to be done to bring a feminist perspective to the everyday work of librarianship. We would love to see this survey methodology extended to include other questions and other participants with different life experiences and perspectives. Research is needed on the ways power is distributed, both formally and informally, in libraries, as well as the ways the profession relies on and benefits from structural racism in our society. We would greatly benefit from studies that evaluate and describe effective models for feminist leadership. And we'd be grateful for more feminist analyses of the biases in the structures and systems that underlie our profession. Truth be told, almost everything in librarianship would benefit from more intersectional feminist analysis.

It is with heartfelt thanks that we acknowledge all of our study participants for the time, openness, vulnerability, and honesty they willingly displayed in working with us on this research.

Bibliography

Accardi, Maria T., ed. *Feminist Pedagogy for Library Instruction.* Sacramento: Library Juice Press, 2013.

Barton, Tracy R. "A Feminist Construction of Leadership in American Higher Education." Ph.D. diss., University of Toledo, 2006. ProQuest (UMI 3264478).

—————. "Feminist Leadership: Building Nurturing Academic Communities." *Advancing Women in Leadership* 22 (2006).

Blackmore, Jill. "Social Justice and the Study and Practice of Leadership in Education: A Feminist History." *Journal of Educational Administration and History* 38, no. 2 (2006): 185-200.

—————. *Troubling Women: Feminism, Leadership, and Educational Change.* Buckingham: Open University Press, 1999.

Bourg, Chris. "The Unbearable Whiteness of Librarianship." *Feral Librarian* (blog). March 3, 2014. https://chrisbourg.wordpress.com/2014/03/03/the-unbearable-whiteness-of-librarianship/.

Brisolara, Sharon. "Feminist Theory: Its Domains and Applications." In *Feminist Evaluation and Research: Theory and Practice*, edited by Sharon Brisolara, Denise Seigart, and Saumitra SenGupta, 3-41. New York: The Guildford Press, 2014.

Chin, Jean Lau. "2003 Division 35 Presidential Address: Feminist Leadership: Feminist visions and Diverse Voices." *Psychology of Women Quarterly* 28 (2004): 1-8.

DeVault, Marjorie L., and Glenda Gross. "Feminist Interviewing: Experience, Talk, and Knowledge." In *Handbook of Feminist Research: Theory and Praxis*, edited by Sharlene Nagy Hesse-Biber, 173-197. Thousand Oaks, CA: SAGE, 2007.

Deyrup, Marta. "Academic Library Leadership, Second-Wave Feminism, and Twenty-First Century Humanism: Reflections on a Changing Profession." In *Leadership in Academic Libraries Today: Connecting Theory to Practice*, edited by Bradford Lee Eden and Jody Condit Fagan, 91-107. Lanham, MD: Rowman & Littlefield, 2014.

Galvan, Angela. "Soliciting Performance, Hiding Bias: Whiteness and Librarianship." *In the Library With the Lead Pipe* (June 3, 2015). http://www.inthelibrarywiththeleadpipe.org/2015/soliciting-performance-hiding-bias-whiteness-and-librarianship/.

Greiner, Joy. "A Comparative Study of the Career Development Patterns of Male and Female Library Administrators in Large Public Libraries." *Library Trends* 34, no. 2 (1985): 259-90.

Hathcock, April. *At the Intersection* (blog). https://aprilhathcock.wordpress.com/.

———. "White Librarianship in Blackface: Diversity Initiatives in LIS." *In the Library With the Lead Pipe* (October 7, 2015). http://www.inthelibrarywiththeleadpipe.org/2015/lis-diversity/.

hooks, bell. *Teaching to Transgress*. New York: Routledge, 1994.

Miner, Kathi N., Toby Epstein Jayaratne, Amanda Pesonen, and Lauren Zurbrügg. "Using Survey Research as a Quantitative Method for Feminist Social Change." In *Handbook of Feminist Research: Theory and Praxis*, by Sharlene Nagy Hesse-Biber. Thousand Oaks, CA: SAGE, 2007.

Olin, Jessica, and Michelle Millet. "Gendered Expectations for Leadership in Libraries." *In the Library With the Lead Pipe* (November 4, 2015). http://www.inthelibrarywiththeleadpipe.org/2015/libleadgender/.

Sadler, Beth, and Chris Bourg. "Feminism and The Future of Library Discovery." *Code4Lib Journal*, no. 28 (April 15, 2015). http://journal.code4lib.org/articles/10425.

Strachan, Jane. "Feminist Educational Leadership: Locating the Concepts in Practice." *Gender and Education* 11, no. 3 (1999): 309-22.

Vinopal, Jennifer. *Library Sphere* (blog). http://vinopal.org/blog/.

———. "The Quest for Diversity in Library Staffing: From Awareness to Action." *In the Library With the Lead Pipe* (January 13, 2016). http://www.inthelibrarywiththeleadpipe.org/2016/quest-for-diversity/

A Feminist Among Us: An Interview with Chris Bourg

Tara Robertson

I'm a big fan of Chris Bourg. I'm inspired by her commitment to social justice, diversity, and feminism. I appreciate the theoretical models she proposes and the concrete ideas she has for making change with a queer feminist agenda. She uses conference keynote invitations as an opportunity to present with and signal boost other opinionated librarians, especially people of color. She embodies the feminist phrase "the personal is political" by being open and vulnerable about parts of her personal life that inform her work.

Currently Chris is the Director of Libraries at MIT. She was the Associate University Librarian for Public Services at Stanford, served as a Battalion Staff Officer in the US Army, and taught at the US Military Academy at West Point. Her influence goes beyond her formal positions. She is very involved in the profession as a keynote speaker at library conferences, the Vice Chair of the Association of Research Libraries' Diversity and Inclusion Committee, and an active contributor on social media.

For someone with her experience and credentials, Chris' humility and openness is refreshing. She posts most of her talks on her website shortly after delivering them, making them accessible to everyone. Chris is one of the few library directors who is active on Twitter engaging with people who work at all levels of libraries.

She is a white woman who talks about systemic racism. She accepts that part of her work is to be patient with other white people who are just starting to see how white supremacy operates in institutions like libraries. Chris' work creates more space for me, a queer, mixed race librarian, to be excited about libraries and social justice, and to imagine and map out a career path in senior management.

Chris and I initially connected on Twitter, and I first met her in person at the Digital Library Federation (DLF) Forum in 2015 in Vancouver. This interview took place over Skype in September 2016. It was a delight and pleasure to interview her for this book.

Tara Robertson: How would you define feminist leadership?

Chris Bourg: That's a great question. I'm almost hesitant to define it. For me one of the key tenets of feminism is the ability to self-identify. I wouldn't want to define leadership for any other feminist. I can tell you that to bring a feminist perspective to my role as a leader involves both some very commonplace, operational aspects and some more theoretical aspects for me.

As an intersectional feminist I try and lead from a perspective of trying to create an organization where people feel comfortable and welcome as their whole authentic selves, to the extent that they want to bring that to work. For me it's a really important way of looking at the workforce. To be honest—and this may sound kind of strange—some of this approach comes out of being in the Army for 10 years. It may seem counterintuitive, but the Army really is a near-total institution where your work and family life are intertwined. Your whole person belongs to the Army. This plays out in all kinds of bad ways, but also in these good ways, where the good leaders really take care of you as a whole person. It's more paternalistic than I am as a library director but that way of thinking about people as whole people, who have lives outside of their job description, is a healthy one. And accepting that people's external lives are not a distraction is just necessary. To ignore this is to ignore part of reality.

Feminism has to do with transparency, agency, and choice. I think about choice as a guiding principle. I want to maximize choice for people—within every decision, in every policy, and in the ways that we do things in this organization. Transparency is also a guiding principle. So much of leadership is about communication. At the leadership level, we often make a decision and then ask the question, "Who should we share this with?"

I want the question to be, "Why shouldn't we share this with everyone?" I want the default to be share with everyone, as soon as possible. If necessary, it's possible to whittle back from there. But if we start with that as the default I think we become more transparent.

Black feminists and feminists of color from the 90s, like bell hooks, Audrey Lorde, Cherríe Moraga and Patricia Hill Collins, inform the way I think about inclusion. It's the practice of looking around the table and literally asking, "Who's missing?" and "How can we more inclusive?" It's also about getting the next level of leadership to ask the same question, and have that spread throughout the organization.

I remember that in your conversation with Lareese Hall[1] at the Association of College and University Libraries, Greater New York Metropolitan Chapter (ACRL/NY) Symposium, you spoke about asking who's missing in terms of staffing, collections and services.[2] You also talked about how Bethany Nowviskie[3] articulated an ethics of care and caring. You connected this ethics of care and caring to the kind of leadership that you learned from the Army.

When I interviewed for this job I was asked "How does running a library differ from being a leader in the Army?" One of the things that happens in the Army is when you take command of a unit you become legally responsible for the health, welfare, and morale of the troops under your command. If you bring that perspective to leadership you have to care about the person and you have to adopt an ethic of caring.

---

1 At the time of ACRL/NY symposium, Lareese Hall was the Architecture and Art Librarian at MIT. At the time of this interview, she is Dean of Libraries at the Rhode Island School of Design.

2 Chris Bourg, "The Radicalism Is Coming from Inside the Library," *Feral Librarian* (blog), December 10, 2015, https://chrisbourg.wordpress.com/2015/12/10/the-radicalism-is-coming-from-inside-the-library/.

3 At the time of this interview, Bethany Nowviskie is the Director of the DLF, at Council on Library and Information Resources and Research Associate Professor of Digital Humanities in the Department of English at the University of Virginia.

It sounds counterintuitive when people think about the Army, until you start to sort of think about the way that in this very sort of male-centric, patriarchal, paternalistic way men talk about their experience in the Army. They talk about being in a band of brothers or about loving their brothers. There is this ethic of love and family that happens there. I like to think that you can take what's good about that and bring it into a more diverse and more progressive culture. At least that's what I'm trying to do.

So how does feminist leadership differ from regular or non-feminist or default style of leadership?

That's a hard question for me, because I don't know how to define the default. In the conversation with Lareese Hall that you mentioned just now, I talked about feminist leadership, and said that other people might call it humanist leadership or progressive leadership and that's OK with me.[4] For me, feminist leadership comes from my grounding in feminist reading and being familiar with and involved in feminist circles.

I think the difference is primarily around priorities, meaning whether you see certain aspects—caring about the whole person, inclusion, agency and paying attention to who's not there—as nice extras or as central to the work. To me, they're central to the work.

I suspect that on some spectrum of feminist to not-feminist leadership, on the far end of the not-feminist spectrum of leadership are those who think that leadership is a neutral endeavor and that a good leader just does what's best for the organization and you accomplish your goals. An anti-feminist or non-feminist style of leadership might assert that feminism has nothing to do with leadership and that leading is neutral. A big tenet of feminist thought is that there is no such thing as neutrality—everyone comes with an agenda. As a feminist, I know that to lead in a way that doesn't pay attention to who's not there, to lead in a way that asserts everything is a meritocracy, or that says I'm not going to worry about the whole person because leading is just about getting the work done—leading in any of these ways is

---

4 Chris Bourg. "Radicalism."

an agenda. Feminist leadership recognizes that all leadership is agenda-driven and is honest about that.

That honesty is really refreshing. There's a post on your blog where you reflect on being explicit about having a queer, feminist agenda.[5]

It's so true. I can't tell you the number of times I give various versions of a talk, and someone says, "Aren't you worried that there may be people in your organization who don't agree with your agenda?" I respond, "Why are you only asking me that?" Many people don't proclaim their agendas, but definitely have agendas, even if they are agendas about maintaining the status quo, and never get asked about how they handle people in their organization who don't agree with their agendas.

Can you pinpoint the time in your career where you became a feminist leader, or was it more of a process?

It's a little of both. I think it definitely was a process but I can pinpoint a time when I became significantly more self-aware that I was leading in that way and that I wanted to and was going to be honest and intentional about it. It had to do with starting to spend some time getting to know some of the women who were working in the library technologies department at Stanford, specifically Bess Sadler.

When Bess came to Stanford and as we got to know each other there was a moment where she was talking to me about the issues facing women in tech. I remember asking "How can I help?" She said conference codes of conduct would really be helpful.

So I had this experience of talking to Bess and other women in the Stanford libraries, and in other libraries, who were willing to be honest about some of the discrimination and sexism and microaggressions that they faced, even in this predominantly female, supposedly liberal profession. And those women, especially Bess, helped me to see the differences, large and small,

---

5 Chris Bourg, "Agendas: Everyone Has One," *Feral Librarian* (blog), August 25, 2013, https://chrisbourg.wordpress.com/2013/08/25/agendas-everyone-has-one/.

that someone in a leadership position could make if they were willing to pay attention to the gender issues.

When I started working with Bess on the paper that we did on feminism and library discovery[6], it really sent me back to some of the feminist literature I had read in the mid 90s, mostly the intersectional feminists of color I mentioned earlier. Re-reading their work got me thinking, "How can I apply these ideas to my life and my role in libraries right now?" It helped me see that so many of the conversations about gender in libraries and in library technology are really mostly about white women, and that we need to be more intentional about thinking about race, sexuality, and other intersecting identities.

I've got to give Bess Sadler a lot of credit. I like to believe that I was being a feminist leader before that, but I wasn't self-conscious about it and intentional about it until those conversations with Bess.

You're an out butch queer woman who's got a very dapper style. I love that you frame these conversation by asking about gender. You're not just asking, "Where are the women?" which often means, "Where are the white women?" You're bringing more complexity to the discussion and I really appreciate that.

It's interesting that you bring that up because one of the first public presentations I gave on gender was a panel on women in library technology. Most of the rest of the panel was straight white women. These straight white women all talked about the problem of being called Mrs., or being asked when they'll get married, or being asked about their kids. They presented these issues as being universal problems for all women. As a butch woman, people don't actually believe I have a daughter, so that's not one of the problems that I face, and I'm never called Mrs. in person, and no one asks me when I'm getting married. That is not the experience of all women.

I have to own the fact that being masculine-presenting gives me some advantages in individual interactions. I can be a feminist.

---

6 Bess Sadler and Chris Bourg, "Feminism and the Future of Library Discovery," *code4lib Journal* 28 (2015), http://journal.code4lib.org/articles/10425.

I can talk about and care about "soft" issues without appearing soft, in a way that traditionally feminine-looking women can't. People know that I have an Army background and expect me to be tough and angry, and to be a certain kind of leader. And because of that and my masculine appearance, I can be more caring and more maternal and I don't get penalized for it in the way that more feminine-looking women, especially white women, do. In fact, I get a lot of credit for it in a way that sometimes men do when they are caring or soft. It's very interesting the ways that these intersections play out.

On your website you have a page stating that your pronouns are she/her/hers[7]. Were you one of the people in libraries who started the practice of putting pronouns in email signatures? That's a small thing but it's also sort of a big thing.

I wish I could take credit for that, but that started with the MIT Libraries Committee on Diversity and Inclusion. They held a workshop for the libraries on how to be a trans ally and this was one of the recommendations. They challenged the library staff to add their pronouns to their email block for 30 days. They talked with me beforehand and I let them know that I'd chime in quickly with my support. Having me, the Director, participate meant that lots of other people did it too. Very few people have changed it back. I will also say that I have gotten questions about it from other Association of Research Libraries (ARL) directors asking about "what's this she/her/hers in your email block?" so it's a great teachable moment. It's really powerful.

You've also written about the challenges in being part of the senior administrative team without being co-opted by the institution. How do you resist being co-opted?

I'm learning that. I haven't figured out the answer yet.

I think somewhere in there is the question, "How do you find allies?" Those questions are very related to me. I have to be completely honest that here at MIT I'm still working on both of

---

7 Chris Bourg. "About Chris," last modified July 23, 2013, accessed November 15, 2016 https://chrisbourg.wordpress.com/about/.

those things. I'm trying to find allies. Because I do think that not being co-opted by the neoliberal impulses of the institution and the bureaucracy is easier if you have allies. Everything is just easier to do when you have allies.

I don't have any peers here. As a library director I am the only library director on my campus. I have peers, rank-wise, but those people have very different jobs from me. The school deans are all doing the same job as each other, just in different disciplines— but in a general way they face a similar set of challenges. But nobody else is running a library on this campus. I think that's hard for anyone in this position. It's meant I've tried to find some of those allies amongst my peers who are fellow library directors. I also rely on my Twitter friends, who are doing library work but generally aren't in leadership positions. When I say "rely on them," I mean I need mirrors. Part of what allies do is they'll tell you when you're being co-opted. I had that at Stanford, to some extent. I'm trying to find that again at MIT. Those relationships are intense and take time to develop. That level of trust doesn't form immediately. Theoretically that's what it would take for me to have a good ally who would hold that mirror up to me.

When I first got here I was trying to say no to a lot of things so that I could really concentrate on learning this job. The things that I did agree to do were the ARL Diversity and Inclusion Committee and a taskforce here at MIT on diversity and inclusion. I have met people on this campus and throughout the ARL who are also committed to this kind of work, which has helped me start to make those relationships, to again have those allies who will hold the mirror up for me.

I have spent so much time in these elite institutions. My whole career has been either in the Army, as a grad student at Stanford, working at Stanford, or working at MIT. I still struggle with the culture of elite institutions, sometimes, but it means that I have had to learn that culture and how to succeed in it. I've learned the language and how the politics work. Ironically, and maybe this is counterintuitive, but for me part of learning how not to get caught by that culture is to flip it and co-opt the bureaucracy for my agenda. At MIT, and I think in other schools throughout the U.S., right now, it's a prime time to be able to do that.

Last fall, with the student protests about race relations at Yale and in Missouri and other places, somehow higher ed was mostly ready to take those issues seriously. They didn't do a great job, but they're not ignoring the problems. They're at least paying lip service, and there are ways to co-opt that lip service for a progressive agenda.

When you were talking about allies it sounded to me like you were talking about community or your people, the people with whom there's trust. You said that it would take time to build that. You began your job at MIT in February 2015, less than 2 years ago. What was it like to uproot and move to a new city at this stage in your career?

Moving at age 50 has been really hard. Making new friends when you're 50 years old is hard!

Social media is huge for me. The people I've been able to meet on social media are my people, my community. In many cases, people I've never met in person and in some cases people I've had the pleasure of meeting at some point. I do feel like there's a whole set of people I know on social media who have my back. But then there are times when I'm trying to get something done, as a library director, and I'm trying to inject that feminist agenda, the diversity and inclusion angle, and I would love to have some advice, but that's not the kind of thing I can tweet out.

I've noticed on social media you've been talking about self-care, exercise and having a good work/life balance. Is taking care of yourself part of a strategy of not being co-opted?

I hadn't thought of it that way but I think it absolutely is, especially being public about it.

There's vulnerability there!

There's vulnerability there in several ways. At MIT, and a little bit at Stanford too, there is this status that you get from being very, very busy and working lots and lots of hours—pulling all-nighters. I suspect that some of my administrative peers at MIT have probably pulled an all-nighter or two. They certainly work ridiculous hours. Being willing to admit that I went on vacation and I didn't check e-mail, and didn't take your call, is a little bit risky. You run the risk of being seen as not as committed. Again, I think that I have a lot of advantages that I'm able to take that risk. I feel pretty secure in my job here. Even if I didn't, I've got a CV that looks pretty good. I don't say that in a cocky way, I've had a lot of privilege and advantage.

There are two parts to the issue of self-care. I absolutely need to do the self-care. I went from playing racquetball twice a week and doing a fair amount of walking and hiking when I was at Stanford to nothing since I got to MIT. In my first year in this job, I went from a pretty active lifestyle to almost completely sedentary. I felt it—in my body and my soul. I finally said "enough is enough" and started being more active. I had to convince myself to start small, because I wanted to get all the way back to racquetball shape in one day.

I guess I was paying attention to some of the staff who work for me who are good at self-care. I learn so much from people with whom I have the privilege of working. I can admire someone for only so long before I realize that if I'm admiring the way they're doing something maybe I could do that thing myself. I bought a Fitbit and I started walking and it's made a big difference.

It goes back again to "What is feminist leadership?" and wanting people to feel welcome as whole people. That includes being supportive of people caring for their whole person, however they need to do that. Being super public about my agenda and who I am means that people keep me accountable. My administrative assistant says, "You say you care about work-life balance, so go home. You have to model it for the rest of us." I needed to model that and I hadn't been doing such a great job of it.

You're a leader within your organization but also within the library community as a whole. Do you operate differently within your organization as compared to within broader library communities like ARL?

I wish I could say I'm the same consistent person, but I'm not. I'm striving to be more integrated, which is a continual journey for me. At Stanford, I was involved in the Taiga leadership forum and I blogged. I think most of the people at Stanford libraries who read my blog were already aligned with me politically. People weren't really paying that much attention unless they already thought it was interesting. Now that I'm the director, staff who read my blog see it as the words of the director, so they're paying more attention. This realization made me want to be more consistent.

I think that I'm bolder sometimes in stuff I do in the profession outside my role in the MIT library. Outside of the MIT libraries, in the talks I give, on Twitter, and wherever else, to some extent I'm trying to be aspirational. As a director I want to be that too, but I also have to be very practical. I also have to be the director and the leader for everyone in the organization, wherever they are in terms of their commitment to social justice or feminist ideals. Whereas outside the libraries, in a lot of the talks I give, I either assume that people are there, or give that talk anyway and let them catch up.

I'm now thinking about the conversation I had with April Hathcock, Scholarly Communications Librarian at New York University, at the National Diversity in Libraries Conference (NDLC). I'm thinking about whose work is it to bring people along. The amount of privilege that I have now, some of which I've always had, means a lot of that work needs to fall on me, and on people like me more broadly. It's easier to be the angry feminist and give that talk but it's probably time for me to pay a little bit more attention to doing that hard work of bringing well-meaning people along.

I do think that I have been significantly more radical off campus than on, but that's becoming less separate. As a director, people here are reading my blog, so it's not like I can separate these spheres, and that's probably a good thing.

So you're saying that outside in the library community you're more aspirational and with your day-to-day job you're more practical. What I think I understood from that is that you have same values but you're dialing them back a little at work.

Yes, I'm dialing it back a little. I think I'm more cautious and strategic about when I show my hand. But at one of our first all-staff meetings, the presentation I gave had my favorite bell hooks quote in it, so I'm not hiding who I am. For the record, the bell hooks quote I shared, revised a bit for libraries, is from *Teaching to Transgress: Education as the Practice of Freedom*:

> The ~~academy~~ *library* is not paradise. But learning is a place where paradise can be created. The ~~classroom~~ *library*, with all its limitations, remains a location of possibility. In that field of possibility we have the opportunity to labor for freedom, to demand of ourselves and our comrades, an openness of mind and heart that allows us to face reality even as we collectively imagine ways to move beyond boundaries, to transgress. This is ~~education~~ *librarianship* as the practice of freedom.[8]

So, within MIT libraries you're trying to be a little more moderate so that you don't alienate your staff? Does being more moderate enable you to do the practical day-to-day sort of management of the library?

I was definitely trying to say that. If I want to lead in an inclusive way I have to make all types of people feel welcome in the organization. Coming in as a big, butch lesbian with a feminist agenda may not feel very inclusive to some people. I'm trying to craft that perspective as inclusive, welcoming, and less aggressive than how I am on social media and in my talks.

We are at an important moment in libraries I think—there's a big cohort of liberal-minded folks who've been working in higher ed leadership for a number of years who are well-intentioned people who have not fully confronted racial privilege. They have not fully confronted how power and privilege play out in the academy. I feel my own impatience, in that I want them to come on get with the program, but I recognize that it will take time.

At NDLC I had an "aha" moment on stage with April Hathcock. I realized it's easier for me to be angry about people who don't get racial privilege and white supremacy. I realized that as a white person, I need to do the hard work of suppressing that anger and playing nice to bring people along. If we want to bring along those well-meaning people, who have the capacity to come along, somebody has to be patient. That is on us white folks.

---

8 Chris Bourg. "Radicalism."

That's also my work as a person who has positional privilege too. It is my job to make these values accessible to everyone in my organization. I'm not saying that everyone is going to come on board but I've got to try to make it accessible. This means I need to take a less aggressive and more patient perspective than I do in the broader library community. Out in social media and in my talks, people are either are going to like it or not and I don't really care. In my organization I have to care.

Sometimes I think the status quo is almost even more insidious than a conservative leadership style because it's presented as being neutral.

I think that in libraries there's a self-identity of being liberal. There's this assumption that the status quo is liberal or progressive enough.

Because librarianship is a predominantly female profession, and people think that feminism is just about women's equality, they think there's not a problem in libraries. The two questions I get when I talk about a feminist agenda are, "What do you do with people who disagree with your agenda, or expect you be neutral?" and "What about the men?"

What do you say in response to "What about the men?"

I'm still working on it. It's always a man who asks something like, "Given that we're a predominantly female profession, what about the problem of underrepresentation of men?" Often I just say that's not a problem I'm particularly concerned about. I'm just not particularly worried about the plight of professional men in this society. That shuts it down; but I've got to come up with a better answer. I need to come up with a more intersectional answer because I am concerned about men of color. There is a dearth of men of color in our organizations. But in general I'm not super worried about the fact that male librarians are in a minority numerically because the stats show that they actually earn higher salaries, anyway. Men also get to leadership positions more quickly.

Are there any points regarding feminist leadership that you want to include in this conversation that we haven't talked about?

One of things that I talked about at the ACRL talk with Lareese Hall is the value of an inclusive, participatory style of leadership.[9] I think this is the way to go long-term but it takes so much longer than traditional leadership styles. It's really a slower process of leadership, and that's not necessarily bad, except that it bumps up against our desire for rapid change. For those who are on board with the agenda, there's a desire to make change quickly because there's a pent-up demand for it.

Here's an example. At Stanford, I was able to get us to adopt a recommendation that our librarians only go to conferences that have a code of conduct. I suggested it to the University Librarian, who had a couple of questions about it. I answered them, and he said yes let's do it, and that was it. That's all it took. And while I like the outcome, the process was not an example of feminist leadership. It was a very top-down decision, and not at all an inclusive process to get to that decision.

When I came to MIT, I said I'd like us to do a similar thing, but I didn't want to be top-down. So it took a year. We formed a committee that gathered lots of input. The statement was drafted by committee. It's a much better statement that is more fully thought out than the one we had at Stanford. This thing that I thought was cool and awesome, and that we did at Stanford quickly, took a year to do at MIT. Feminist leadership is slow leadership.

So, if feminist leadership is a slow process, what does feminist succession planning look like?

I worry that being a progressive feminist is in some ways in contradiction with being a leader in a bureaucracy. These jobs are leadership jobs in bureaucracies. So many of the amazing librarians, archivists, and others that I know who work in libraries are feminists who are super progressive, brilliant and active, and who have no desire to move up the chain of command and become leaders in library organizations. I really worry about that.

---

9 Chris Bourg, "Radicalism."

I think that one way of trying to make these jobs more attractive is by creating a sense of openness, making it clear that you can be a feminist and you can hold on to your values. You can be a feminist and be in these jobs and it can be very rewarding. I want to make these jobs attractive to more junior librarians who share these values. One of the reasons I am so open about my work and about the fact that I try to bring these feminist values to my job as a library director is that I hope in some small way to show others that it is possible to be a feminist leader in libraries. I want progressive, feminist, radical, anti-racist folks in this profession to be able to see themselves as library directors and other senior leaders in our libraries and our profession. Ultimately, that's why I agreed to give this interview and why I'm so excited about this book.

Bibliography

Bourg, Chris. "About Chris" last modified July 23, 2013, accessed November 15, 2016 https://chrisbourg.wordpress.com/about/.

———. "Agendas: Everyone Has One," *Feral Librarian* (blog), August 25, 2013, https://chrisbourg.wordpress.com/2013/08/25/agendas-everyone-has-one/.

———. "The Radicalism Is Coming from Inside the Library," *Feral Librarian* (blog), December 10, 2015, https://chrisbourg.wordpress.com/2015/12/10/the-radicalism-is-coming-from-inside-the-library/.

Sadler, Bess and Chris Bourg, "Feminism and the Future of Library Discovery," *code4lib Journal* 28 (2015), http://journal.code4lib.org/articles/10425

About the Contributors

Dale Askey is Associate University Librarian, Library & Learning Technologies and the Administrative Director of the Lewis & Ruth Sherman Centre for Digital Scholarship at McMaster University. He received a Master of Arts in German in 1995, a Master of Information Science and Learning Technologies in 1998, and is currently completing his PhD at the Humboldt University in Berlin writing on the post-war German community in Czechoslovakia.

Jennifer Askey holds a PhD in Germanic Languages and Literatures from Washington University in St. Louis and was formerly Associate Professor of German at Kansas State University. Her research focused on girls and reading and she has taught German, Children's Literature, and Women's Studies at several universities in the United States and Canada. Currently, she is the sole proprietor of Energized Academic, an academic life and career coaching business. As a coach, she works with her clients to align their jobs and career paths with their values, to live a life that honors their values in the world.

Rachel Fleming is Collections Initiatives Librarian at the University of Tennessee at Chattanooga. Fleming received a Master of Arts degree in Library Science from the University of Missouri – Columbia in 2006 and a Bachelor of Arts in History from Grinnell College. Fleming has library experience in collection development, collection assessment, acquisitions, and serials management. Fleming is a co-blogger, creating the Unified Library Scene at unifiedlibraryscene.blogspot.com.

April Hathcock is the Scholarly Communications Librarian at NYU where she educates the campus community on issues of ownership, access, and rights in the research lifecycle. She received her J.D. and LL.M. in International and Comparative Law from Duke University School of Law and her MLIS from the University of South Florida. Before entering librarianship, she practiced intellectual property and antitrust law for a global private firm. She is an intersectional feminist whose research interests include cultural creation and exchange and the ways in which social and legal infrastructures benefit the works of certain groups over others.

Shana Higgins is Interim Director of Armacost Library at the University of Redlands. She received a Master of Arts in Latin American & Caribbean Studies and a Master of Library Science, both in 2006 from Indiana University, Bloomington. She currently lives in the Inland Empire, a region in Southern California, surrounded by the rugged San Bernardino Mountains and rapidly multiplying mega-warehouses.

Shirley Lew is the Dean, Library, Teaching & Learning Services at Vancouver Community College. She has a Bachelor of Arts in Human Geography and a Master of Library and Information Studies, both from the University of British Columbia. She is active in the local literary community and serves as a Director on the Board of Vancouver Writers Fest. She lives and works where she was born and raised, in the city of Vancouver on the unceded traditional lands of Musqueam, Sḵwxwú7mesh, and Tsleil-Waututh people.

Safiya Umoja Noble is an assistant professor in the Department of Information Studies in the Graduate School of Education and Information Studies at UCLA. She also holds appointments in the Departments of African American Studies, Gender Studies, and Education. Her research on the design and use of applications on the Internet is at the intersection of race, gender, culture, and technology. She is currently working on a monograph on racist and sexist algorithmic bias in search engines like Google (forthcoming, NYU Press). She currently serves as an Associate Editor for the *Journal of Critical Library and Information Studies*, and is the co-editor of two books: *The Intersectional Internet: Race, Sex,*

Culture and Class Online (Peter Lang, Digital Formations, 2016), and Emotions, Technology & Design (Elsevier, 2015). Safiya holds a PhD and MS in Library & Information Science from the University of Illinois at Urbana-Champaign, and a BA in Sociology from California State University, Fresno with an emphasis on African American/Ethnic Studies.

Kelly Rhodes McBride is Associate Professor and Coordinator of Information Literacy and Instruction at Appalachian State University. She holds a Masters in Information Sciences from the University of Tennessee and an Education Specialist degree from Appalachian State University. Her expertise includes student learning outcomes assessment, and information literacy. Current research interests include diversity in librarianship, affective learning in library instruction, and the intersection of social media and information literacy.

Lisa Richmond is Director of Library and Archives at Wheaton College, a board member of the Canadian Association of Professional Academic Librarians, and co-editor of the *Canadian Journal of Academic Librarianship.* She graduated from the University of British Columbia with an MLIS degree and from Regent College in Vancouver, BC, with an MA in theology. She is currently enrolled as a PhD student in seventeenth-century French literature at the University of Montpellier in France.

Maura A. Smale is Chief Librarian and Department Chair at New York City College of Technology (City Tech), CUNY, where she works with library faculty and staff to support the City Tech community in our academic pursuits. She holds a PhD in Anthropology from New York University and an MLIS from Pratt Institute, and has served as Co-Director of the City Tech OpenLab, an open digital platform for teaching, learning, and collaboration. Her research interests include undergraduate academic culture, critical librarianship, educational technologies, and game-based learning.

Tara Robertson is the Accessibility Coordinator at the Centre for Accessible Post-secondary Education Resources British Columbia (CAPER-BC). She is a librarian who who doesn't work in a library. She loves figuring out how things work, why they break, and how to make them work better. Tara has been a librarian for 10 years and a feminist for a lot longer. Her other interests include universal design, accessibility, open source software and intellectual freedom. You can find her on Twitter at @ tararobertson or at www.tararobertson.ca.

Jennifer Vinopal is Associate Director for Information Technology at The Ohio State University where she is responsible for the staff and work of the Digital Initiatives, Applications Development and Support, and Infrastructure Support departments. Her professional background is in humanities scholarship, library collection development, digital library and digital scholarship initiatives, and public service. Her research examines various aspects of organizational culture, including methods for communication and strategic planning, management practices for building scalable and sustainable services, the quest for diversity in the library profession, and the value and praxis of intersectional feminist leadership.

Baharak Yousefi is Head of Library Communications at Simon Fraser University. She serves as Director on the Board of British Columbia Libraries Cooperative and is a member of the Advisory Board of Kwi Awt Stelmexw. She received a Master of Arts in Women's Studies in 2003 from Simon Fraser University and a Master of Library and Information Studies in 2007 from University of British Columbia. She lives on the unceded lands of the Musqueam, Sḵwxwú7mesh, and Tsleil-Waututh people in Vancouver, BC.

Index

CPSIA information can be obtained
at www.ICGtesting.com
Printed in the USA
BVOW11s2011251017
498611BV00021BA/459/P